# The Unmumsy Mum A–Z
## AN INEXPERT GUIDE TO PARENTING

# THE UNMUMSY MUM A–Z

## AN INEXPERT GUIDE TO PARENTING

Sarah Turner

BANTAM PRESS

TRANSWORLD PUBLISHERS
61–63 Uxbridge Road, London W5 5SA
www.penguin.co.uk

Transworld is part of the Penguin Random House group of companies
whose addresses can be found at global.penguinrandomhouse.com

First published in Great Britain in 2019 by Bantam Press
an imprint of Transworld Publishers

Illustrations by Alyana Cazalet

A CIP catalogue record for this book
is available from the British Library

ISBN 9781787632172

Typeset in 12/14.5 pt Dante MT Pro
by Integra Software Services Pvt. Ltd, Pondicherry

Printed and bound in Great Britain by Clays Ltd, Elcograf S.p.A.

Penguin Random House is committed to a sustainable
future for our business, our readers and our planet. This book
is made from Forest Stewardship Council® certified paper.

1 3 5 7 9 10 8 6 4 2

*For Sophie Christopher*
*It's not the same without you x*

The Turner family: Henry, James, Jude, Sarah and Wilf

# Introduction

ABC. Simple as 123. *Unless* you're writing an A–Z and discover you're a thirty-something mother of three who can't remember the order of the alphabet without mentally singing the alphabet song from the beginning, while using fingers to work out which letter comes next. I must have done that a thousand times during the writing of this book and I *still* have to think twice about whether N comes before or after M. There was also a period somewhere in the middle of the writing process when I became so consumed by thoughts of the trickier letters, worried I would end up with gaps, that I found myself randomly shouting, 'Yes, that's it! V is for Vasectomy! Get in!' – much to the confusion of other mums on the school run.

If you've followed me online and/or read either of my previous two books, you'll know that this is the third book in the *Unmumsy Mum* series (though if you've not read the others, don't panic, it doesn't matter!). What you might not know is that this is to be the last *Unmumsy Mum* book, at least for the time being. I can't, of course, rule out returning to write *Unmumsy Reloaded: The Teenage Years* in ten years' time, full of tales about underage drinking and dilemmas over whether you should say something when you put tissues in your boys' rooms or just write 'instead of the sock' on a Post-it note. For now, though, this is it.

I wrote the best part of the previous books at home on my bed – something I was once forced to explain, with a red face, after Henry told an adult in a professional setting that Mummy 'earns money on her laptop in bed', as though I were some kind of webcam girl. I would be terribly disappointing as a webcam girl, unless someone happened to have a fetish for mums in dressing-gowns dipping Pom-Bears into hummus (which, if you didn't know, is a taste sensation).

This book, though, was largely written from a desk in a co-working office and, while that's certainly an upgrade from the bedroom in terms of the creative environment, it does have the potential to get a touch awkward if people in the office don't know what you're working on. On only my second day, having been brainstorming ideas, I went to make a cup of tea and returned to my desk to find I'd left the words 'Guilt', 'Mental health', 'Ikea' and 'Vagina' on my screen, which I'm sure, out of context, made for an alarming list. I've also remained too scared to enquire about linking my laptop to a printer, in case Chris three desks down unwittingly finds himself reading about my fanny dramas when he was expecting to pick up some detailed architectural drawings.

I have put my everything into this book and tried my hardest to repay the good fortune I've been afforded in being allowed to escape the house two days a week to write it. A bit like my third baby, this third book is different from the two that came before it, and I hope it's special in its own right. I feel I should point out now, in case you are hoping this is going to be a serious A–Z reference book with sections on eczema and how best to discipline a toddler, that what follows does not contain a huge amount of practical wisdom, or in fact anything practical at all. However, with any luck, it might just make you laugh and, more than anything else, I hope it reassures you that, whatever it *looks* like, all parents are just muddling along, really, doing our best at what sometimes feels like an impossible job.

# A&E

Though never somewhere you want to find yourself at 9 p.m. on a Monday, the chances are, at some stage, it's where you are going to find yourself at 9 p.m. on a Monday. This is because children are stupid. They do stupid things, they put things in stupid places and they trip over things you asked them to tidy away 'before someone gets hurt'. During the writing of this book, an otherwise unremarkable Monday evening turned into a high-drama episode of *Casualty* when our Henry tripped over in his bedroom, in the dark. He was supposed to be in bed but had ventured downstairs to give us the latest in a long line of reasons why he couldn't get to sleep. This time it was Lord

Voldemort's fault. He couldn't sleep because he was scared Lord Voldemort was hiding in the house waiting to do a Killing Curse on him (curiously, he's only scared of Lord Voldemort on school nights, when he's not allowed to stay up as late). Of course, we gave him a cuddle and offered some soothing words – 'Voldemort can't get you here, darling, because White Teddy is next to you and he has an impenetrable force field' – then we pushed him back up the stairs and told him not to bother us again unless it was urgent.

Approximately thirty seconds later we heard a thud, a shout and then blood-curdling screaming, quite unlike any sound he's ever produced. James was first on the scene, racing up the stairs before declaring, 'Sar! There's blood everywhere!', at which I flapped around grabbing tea towels and shouting, 'Calm down!' for no real reason other than it's what I'm most used to shouting. Henry then appeared at the bottom of the stairs with blood pouring from his face. Honestly, it was *everywhere*. I thought at first that he must have fallen and broken his nose but soon established, as he managed to get the words out through panicked sobs, that he had, in fact, tripped and face-planted on the spiky bit of Batman's Batcave, which had left an impressive hole in his face between his eyebrows.

Reassuring a whimpering child that they're not going to die as they hold their hands up and scream, 'My hands! There's blood on my hands!' like a tiny Macbeth in Marvel pyjamas is hard to do when your own expression is one of panic. I'm a little ashamed to admit that the second thought I had, after checking that he hadn't lost an eye, was whether or not I'd have time to Vanish the carpet before leaving for the hospital – those first few hours are crucial for getting the worst of the stain out. This probably accounted for at least half of the panic on my face.

I tried to say the right things: *The blood makes it seem worse than it is. We'll pop to A&E just to get it checked. Don't worry, Best*

*Friend* [his favourite bear] *can have a wash when we get back.* I
then resorted to the only parenting tool that has thus far never
let me down – I grabbed a bag of Haribo Giant Strawbs out of
the cupboard as an incentive to get him in the car and to keep
him calm in the waiting room.

I needn't have worried about packing snacks to soothe him
at the hospital because it turned out he found A&E very exciting
indeed. The horror of the incident at home soon evolved into
a momentous storytelling opportunity. He spoke very loudly
and deliberately about the bloodstains on his pyjamas and every
now and again said, 'I think I feel a bit dizzy,' with one hand to
the head, as he continued to shove Giant Strawbs into his gob
with the other. Even when he was being glued back together he
was chatting about 'all the blood' and at regular intervals he
would ask, 'What time is it now, Mum?' then punch the air in
triumph at the fact he was up so late on a school night.

Aside from the genuinely very poorly people in A&E, we
came across a little girl who had trapped her fingers in a drawer
(one her mum had warned her not to play with) and a little boy
of around three who had casually announced to his dad at
teatime that he had Blu-Tack in both ears, which he'd pushed
in a bit earlier. They're a different breed, kids. Quite
extraordinary.

I'd love to report that my little chat with Henry on the way
home about why I ask them to keep their rooms tidy and
why it's important they at least keep their floors clear ('I
don't say these things for fun') was taken on board, but it's
still muggins here who is kicking toys under their beds every
evening to avoid a repeat performance.

The carpet survived, in case you're wondering. Though I
have to say there was a good week or so when I feared my
search history, including 'How to get bloodstains out of carpets', would lead the police to our door.

As for the injury, we were incredibly lucky he landed exactly where he did and not an inch either side, which means there is no long-term damage, though we have been told he's likely to end up with a permanent scar, something he's rather keen on, as he thinks it will make him look like Harry Potter. A fitting end to the incident, really, given he was only out of bed in the first place because Lord Voldemort had given him the willies.

# Admin

I remember joining The Real World straight from university and feeling aggrieved that I was expected to sort out things like life insurance, council tax and MOTs in my spare time, on top of all the work-based admin I was ploughing through nine to five. There was always *something* that needed doing – an appointment that needed booking, a form that needed filling, someone who needed paying. 'We need a PA!' I'd chuckle to my then fiancé (now husband), both of us tickled by how much paperwork and organisation adulthood had brought with it. Weren't we *busy*?!

Fast-forward a decade, to the home we now share with three charming, if slightly feral, small people we made ourselves, and we need more than a PA. In fact, I'm sure we could advertise for a full team of staff to manage all the extra admin parenting has brought with it and still have tasks outstanding. We'd have to employ someone in the team solely to manage school-party invites and, preferably, if their hours would allow, take the kids to the parties as well (time and a half for soft-play parties, obviously).

I don't remember the *baby* admin being quite so bad, just so long as you remembered to keep hold of the little red book with the chart in it that tells you whether your child is too small, a porker or 'just right' (we had two thin ones and a chunkier one, but it was OK because they were all 'following the line' from birth so we were allowed to keep them). There was the odd letter that required action – immunisations that needed booking and such like – but they were quick jobs. No dramas.

It felt as though we were dropping a lot of balls when Henry started school and we were suddenly hit with prompts about book-club money, harvest-festival donations, cake-baking/faking, non-uniform days ('Don't forget £1!') and endless raffle tickets, but I don't think the admin shit *really* hit the fan until we'd had a third baby and were simultaneously trying to manage the school admin alongside Jude's nursery admin, on next to no sleep. We'd find ourselves missing the memo about class photographs and only find out on the day as we pushed a dishevelled-looking Henry through the door with a Weetos stain on his jumper.

I did my best to keep up with the important things and booked Henry and Jude a dentist appointment, which James took them along to, only to discover that I had, in fact, booked an appointment for *me* and Henry and, worse still, Jude wasn't even registered, which resulted in a stern telling-off about missing appointments (to pass back to me) and Jude wailing, 'But Mum said I could have my teeth checked!' all the way home.

As the kids continue to get older and the parenting admin increases further (and hiring a PA is not a realistic solution to our diary-management ineptitude), I think we're just going to have to get better at remembering to do things. It might be wise to start by getting one of those family organisers you stick on the wall, rather than continuing with our current system, which is to stuff letters and reminders between the toaster and the spaghetti jar and do bugger all about any of it. The problem is, I'm too scared to look there now.

# Appraisal

There are no appraisals in Parentland. No end-of-year grading, no performance-development review where you sit down with a line manager to look over a grid of all your professional strengths and weaknesses. How many times over the years had I cobbled together some absolute bollocks about where I was succeeding in my job and what I hoped to achieve over the next twelve months? It was usually total waffle, frantically typed and printed out minutes before the meeting. Occasionally, it would be accompanied by the odd email I'd saved from a customer who was bigging me up, or a colleague who wanted to thank me for doing something that was arguably part of my job anyway, because I knew I'd be asked to provide examples of specific 'competencies' deemed necessary to achieve a certain grade. A tick-box exercise. A waste of everyone's time. Or so I thought.

It was several months later, as I was kneeling on the floor of the kitchen deconstructing a pram so I could use a toothbrush to clean vomit out of fabric creases I couldn't otherwise reach, that it occurred to me that there is no such competency framework for parenting. No annual debrief of your accomplishments. Yes, there are sporadic opportunities for feedback along the way (often when you are unprepared and least expecting it), but it's not the same as being *appraised*. Nobody sits you down and says, 'What do you think you have done well this week/month/year?' No one helps you set parental-development goals for the next twelve months. If they did, I would have saved the pram deep-clean as an example of going 'above and beyond'.

Instead, it's all too easy for the days to roll into weeks without anyone reminding you that you're doing a good job – and the absence of that recognition can leave you feeling like you haven't achieved very much. Imagine if you *were* forced to attend a performance review a couple of times a year. Granted, it would be a bit of a ball ache, undoubtedly a little bit cringe, but the opportunity to jot down examples of things you feel you've been doing well, alongside those you have found a challenge, might be a healthy one:

- *I have demonstrated perseverance by washing and changing the cot bedding every day, despite knowing the baby will coat his fresh sheets in a reflux shower within seconds.*

- *Whatever circus unfolds beforehand, I finish the day with a story and an 'I love you' at bedtime.*

- *I manage to keep all swearing under my breath when the kids insist on watching the abomination that is 'Ryan ToysReview' on YouTube – a huge challenge given that pretty much everything about that channel grinds my gears: the fact that it should logically be called 'Ryan's Toy Review', the impossibly high pitch of Ryan's mum's voice and the depressing knowledge that I'll never be as rich as a seven-year-old whose face is plastered on plastic 'surprise' eggs in toy shops around the globe.*

- *When my three-year-old sniffed his Smelly Mummy Pig comforter so much that her foot fell off, I stepped up to the plate and sewed it back on.*

The last one is performance-related-bonus territory, I'm sure of it.

It would probably be taking things too far to draw up your own appraisal document and email it across to the health visitor asking for their comments ahead of the two-year check, but if you're ever feeling underappreciated, just remember that if you *were* asked what you do well or to justify why you are the best person for the job, you absolutely could.

A pay rise is still unlikely, though, more's the pity.

# Awake

As a parent, you'll spend a much higher percentage of your life awake than you ever did BC (before children). Late nights, midnight raving, crawling into bed at 5 a.m. – these things will continue but, unlike the old days, 'raving' now means doing the big-fish-little-fish forearm dance to the sick beats of Ewan the Dream Sheep, and crawling occurs not because the room is spinning and you're worried about your lamb shish from King Kebab reappearing but because going to ground, commando-style, is the only way you can avoid detection as you attempt to escape the bedroom of a toddler whose spidey senses kick in the moment he can no longer feel your breath by his head.

When you have your first child, friends and family will tell you to 'sleep when the baby sleeps', but you won't. Instead, you'll feel like you ought to be maximising that quiet time to tidy up or cook a meal or, on rarer occasions, have a hot cuppa in front of a boxset (which you won't actually watch because a quick browse of something on your phone will snowball, until you find yourself three pages deep into a Mumsnet thread initiated by a woman who caught her husband knocking one out to *Game of Thrones*: 'AIBU* to call this cheating?'). If you go on to have more children, you'll almost certainly wish you could go back and slap your first-time-parent self in the face with a wet muslin for *not* napping when the baby napped, something you've been fantasising about doing since baby two joined the fold but can't act on because baby one grew into a toddler who, if left unattended, puts phone chargers and other small electrical items into the washing machine.

. . . . . . . . . . . . .

* Am I Being Unreasonable? (Generally, the answer is yes, they are.)

BC, you might have been an eight-hours-a-night kind of person with an extra doze at weekends, but it's usually not long before those sleep expectations are lowered, and then lowered some more, until anything greater than two hours is deemed a decent chunk. In fact, it now seems nothing sort of preposterous that you used to indulge in almost *five hundred minutes* of sleep. In one go! How extravagant.

As the kids get older, they'll hopefully grow out of having to be fed several times during the night, but that doesn't mean you'll get back to your eight-hour stretches. Midnight interruptions will simply shift into wet beds, nightmares, panics over misplaced teddies and urgent questions such as 'When we get our cat, can we call him Hulk Hogan?' (despite you having made it clear several times that getting a cat is not on the cards) and 'How long does it take to count to 1 billion?' Out of desperation, you will indulge their pressing query and end up confirming, through a yawn, that the first Google page you landed on suggested it would take somewhere in the region of thirty years to count to a billion, *now go the f\*\*k to sleep.*

You'll come to realise that, far from being two distinct states, as you had previously believed, there's actually a vast spectrum between what it means to be awake and what it means to be asleep. It's quite possible to exist in a brain fog somewhere in the middle. A whole continuum of alertness you never knew existed, ranging from 'reasonably with it after a coffee' to 'complete zombie, micro-napping at the dinner table'. Is it day? Is it night? Have you eaten? Have you got pants on? Who knows? It's the body's equivalent of power-saving mode – your performance is limited, your brightness is reduced, you take longer to process updates, but you still work at a basic level. Just keep going.

# Baby Brain

Every so often, an article about 'baby brain' does the rounds, prompting a debate about whether it's really 'a thing' or whether, in fact, it's a load of old codswallop/an excuse for mums-to-be to get away with being a bit useless for three quarters of a year. I seem to recall reading something last year about how scientists had proven that a loss of grey matter really does occur in pregnant women, thus explaining the so-called baby-brain phenomenon.

However, I'm not about to mourn the grey matter I lost during pregnancy, thrice. Instead, what I want to know is where all my grey matter is *now*? More than a year into the third-baby adventure, and I still seem to have lost the plot. RIP plot. Last seen in 2017. Probably. I can't remember, because all sense of plot has been lost.

The legendary baby-brain traits have been out in full force since Wilf was born. In isolation, these things are just a bit daft, but when you start adding them up you reach the sum total of a woman who is not managing to 'adult' very well. My husband has been looking at me with a face of bewilderment, never more so than when a package of new pillowcases arrived that I must have ordered (but had forgotten I'd ordered) during a night feed. I'd ordered sixteen plain white pillowcases. I still have no idea why. Then there was the day we needed something from town and, as we left the house, he said, 'I've got Wilf, the pram and all our coats, have you got the change bag?'

'Yes, darling,' I told him, 'I've got the change bag.'

We parked up, got out of the car and put the baby in the pram. We didn't have the change bag. We went home.

I've also attempted to change gear at a roundabout (we've had an automatic for two years), made myself several cups of tea using cold water from the kettle, turned up on the wrong day for several appointments and had the mother of all panics that my Instagram had been hacked and the hackers had changed my password before remembering that *I* had changed my password, three weeks before. My bunch of keys, which includes our car key, is regularly left in the front door, which James reminds me means someone could rob us, kill us then steal the car without any hassle. It's as though my mind is permanently 'elsewhere', only I don't think it actually goes anywhere, it's just hibernating.

It can't be a hormonal thing after this long, can it? I can't even really blame it on sleep deprivation any more because, unlike the first few months (aka 'The Fog'), the boys mostly sleep through the night now, and yet I still can't remember the last time I felt truly rested. I always feel frazzled. Maybe that's all it is. Perhaps prolonged baby brain is simply the conse-quence of never rejuvenating all the grey matter you shed dur-ing pregnancy – it doesn't have the space to rejuvenate because in its place sits all the day-to-day crap you're now preoccupied with. Whether there is a proven biological reason for it or not, I'm calling it: baby brain exists and can last a long time. Possibly even a lifetime. What was I saying again?

# Bickering

The following is a transcript from a recent car journey that I feel perfectly encapsulates the ridiculousness of my children's bickering.

**Henry:** [angrily] 'You're fired. I am *firing* you.'

**Jude:** [upset] 'No, I am not fired, Henry!'

**Henry:** 'You *are* fired, Jude. I told you that at Nanny's. Stop saying you're not fired!'

**Jude:** [crying, waking a sleeping Wilf up]: 'I'm not fired, Henry! Muuuuuuuum! Henry keeps saying I'm fired, but I'm not fired.'

**Me:** [massaging my temples in the front passenger seat] 'Henry, can you stop winding your brother up, please?'

**Henry:** 'I'm not winding him up!' [whispers to Jude] 'You are fired, though.'

**Jude:** 'He's said it again! Stop saying it, Henry! You're the worst person in my life.'

**Me:** [over the noise of Wilf's crying] 'Can we all just calm down a bit, please. Henry – what exactly are you firing Jude from?'

**Henry:** 'Double secret club. You know, like I have at school. Jude's not in it.'

**Jude:** [whacking Henry in the leg] *'I AM in it, Henry!'*

**Henry:** 'Ow! Not the double secret club, you're not. I'm in charge, and you're fired. Mum, Jude hit me because I said he was fired.'

**Me:** [through gritted teeth] 'Don't hit your brother, Jude. Does it really matter about secret club? Can you not make up your own secret club? I'll be in it with you.'

**Jude:** [sobbing] 'I wanted to be in the double secret club, and now I hate Henry. He's the worst person in my life.'

**Henry:** 'You're the worst person in *my* life. You're a doofus!'

**Jude:** 'You're a doofus! Mum, Henry called me a doofus!'

**Me:** 'Do not say another word to each other until we are home or I'll ban all secret clubs.' [crying from all three children, all the way home]

# Birds and Bees

I wasn't prepared for the kids to have an awareness of sex quite so early. I like to think we're a pretty liberal household, and I've always wanted the boys to grow up knowing that they can chat freely about anything without shame or embarrassment. However, I also thought we'd have a few more years before 'doing it' was brought up as a topic of conversation at the dinner table. I'd assumed, mistakenly, that it would be something we'd have a bit of a heads-up about, perhaps a letter home from school saying, 'We're going to be talking about sex this week.' With any luck, that lesson would be an improvement on the excruciating sex-education session *I* had when I was at school, when a red-faced teacher wheeled the VHS player into the assembly hall and we watched a baby crowning. I think it was less sex education and more a deterrent message: *Never have sex because, if you do, you'll have to birth a baby, and look how bad that is.* I think there might also have been some cartoon sperm somewhere and then, to round it off, we sat and passed sanitary towels around in a circle, which the boys howled at. *Any questions?* Nope. Job done. We were now fully informed to not have sex and none the wiser about periods.

Of course, there was no such communication home from school on this occasion because it wasn't the teachers who'd been telling Henry about sex, it was a classmate who'd 'heard it off his sister'. It was a Tuesday teatime, spaghetti Bolognese had just been served and Jude was busy picking out the 'bits'. We'd been talking about someone we'd seen on the telly who had an interesting job and it had prompted us to ask the boys what they thought they might like to do when they're older. This in turn started a conversation about them as adults – perhaps they would fall in love and have babies of their own. It was then that Henry said, 'I don't ever want to do sexing with anyone.'

I just wasn't expecting it and did a kind of cough-splutter, where some Bolognese shot out my mouth. What was the right thing to say here?

'Erm, OK. What do you know about "sexing" then?'

'I'm not telling you, but you have to use willies and bums. It's disgusting.'

This time it was James who coughed and spluttered. We exchanged glances. *Willies and bums?* Crikey, it had all got very liberal indeed. Jude, by this point, was laughing his head off at the mention of willies, and Henry was looking worried, as though he feared he had got something wrong. I knew I had to tread carefully with what I said next and try to help him make sense of it.

'If you're making a baby, then it would involve willies and *vaginas* – or fannies, or whatever you choose to call lady bits – rather than willies and bottoms, sweetheart.'

He replied, with a face of horror, 'Well, that's even *worse*! And you two must have done sexing three times!'

To which I laughed and James replied, 'That's about the measure of it, son.'

So now, out of nowhere, our seven-year-old knows that we have, in the past, done some sexing. Certainly not willies and bums, though.

# Boasting

'Being proud of my kids doesn't mean I'm *boasting*.' I was eaves-dropping on a conversation between two mums at Bounce and Rhyme. *Damn straight*, I thought, as I balanced a baby Henry on my lap and got ready to Wind the Bobbin Up. 'I mean, it's only natural to want to share your little ones' achievements with others. That doesn't make you *boasty*, does it?'

As the session unfolded and Henry continued to show zero interest in acting out the plight of poor Incy Wincy, who'd almost drowned several times but nevertheless persisted in climbing up the water spout, I started to understand why someone might have told Mrs Definitely-not-boasting that she was, in fact, a bit boastful. It started with the clapping. Her friend's baby, though mesmerised by the *clap, clap, clapping* during 'Wind the Bobbin Up', wasn't making any attempt to join in with the clapping herself. 'I wouldn't worry,' the not-one-to-brag mum said, 'Most babies can't clap until they're eight or nine months old, so she's not *behind*. She'll get there in her own time! I think our Phoebe was just super-advanced with her clapping – have you seen how co-ordinated she is?! So clever.'

When it was time for the instruments to come out, Phoebe's mum launched into a commentary on how well baby Phoebe could shake a maraca in time to the music. Then, at the very end of the session, just as the other mum started yawning and complaining about 'another sleepless night', she smiled with concern then said, 'Do you think it's because she sleeps in with you, though? I can't imagine shar-ing our bed with Phoebe, but then she's been sleeping through since she was eight weeks!' I realised, in that moment, that there is a fine line between being proud of your child's achievements and being a bit of a tosser.

**B**

Six years on, and I've met plenty more mums like Phoebe's, in a variety of contexts. The common denominator, and what, in my opinion, means they've crossed the line from understandably proud parent into Boasty McBoastface territory, is when said pride is likely to leave the other parent feeling a bit flat. Particularly if that other parent has commented on something their child is not doing, or having trouble doing, and The Boaster follows it up with a run-down of how *their* child is absolutely bossing it.

Still, Phoebe's mum's boasting, though a little insensitive, at least appeared to have its roots in genuine triumphs – her baby really did have a good command of the maracas and her clapping was impressive. Even more intolerable than parental boasting is when it's total *bullshit*. Those mums and dads who are on a crusade of one-upmanship. Anything your kid can do, their kid can do better, and faster, and definitely sooner.

You might be proud of your tiny human for learning the alphabet (glossing over the fact they think 'elemenopee' is one letter), but just know The Bullshitter's tiny human can recite the alphabet *backwards*. In Portuguese. If your baby started sleeping through at seven months, their baby started sleeping through as an egg. Spend too long standing next to them and you'll hear all about how their three-year-old was scouted at Diddikicks football practice and has since been signed up to play for a Premiership club (do not challenge them on this, even if you're fairly sure the 'scout' they mentioned was Jim the caretaker; it's just not worth it). You'll know deep down that they're talking rubbish, but it can still be hard to ignore the constant hype they create about their children and consequently very easy to believe that your child, who spent most of Diddikicks licking rather than kicking the football, is destined for a life of talentless

22

mediocrity. Just remember that bullshit almost always starts to smell in the end.

# Boundaries

These are things you must enforce with your children if you want them to respect you.

No, us neither.

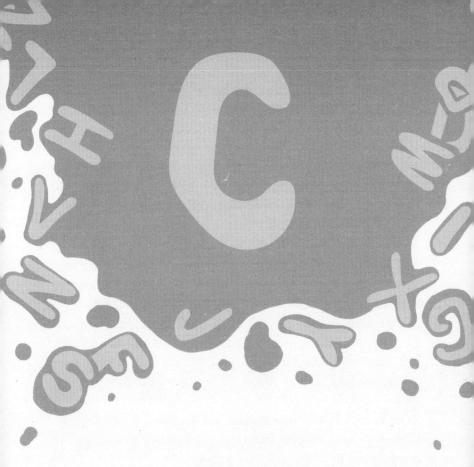

# Classes

Three children in to the parenting adventure and I'm still on the fence as to whether baby and toddler classes are a total sanity saver or the most ridiculous thing you could put yourself through. I think perhaps a bit of both. I'm not talking about the playgroups or parent-and-baby sessions where you can just rock up for a bit of Play-Doh action and a nursery-rhyme sing-along; I'm talking about the ones where your baby is actually expected to *do* an activity or learn something.

Any excuse to get showered, dressed and out of the house is a welcome one and there will usually be other adults there to chat to, the value of which cannot be underestimated, particularly if you'd otherwise be talking to yourself all day. However, unlike the playgroup drop-ins that generally cost no more than a couple of quid (and include a biscuit), these more structured lessons or groups can be quite pricey. How much bang you get for your buck will depend on how your child responds to the activity you're attempting. Do they join in? Do they appear to be enjoying themselves? Our experience of the baby/toddler class environment, so far, has been a mixed bag, ranging from 'Shit, he hates it' (baby massage) and 'I don't care if he's not singing, there are nice mums here who might let me be friends with them' (Monkey Music) to 'I actually think he likes this one, he's got a natural flair for performing, which he obviously gets from me' (Pyjama Drama). Incredibly, we have managed to produce not one, not two, but *three* children who wear a face which says, 'What the fuck is this?' whenever we take them to something new, but I have learned that things usually improve – you just have to stick it out for a bit and not succumb to the temptation of pulling a sickie from the class you've paid termly in advance for.

Most recently, we embarked on Turtle Tots baby-swimming lessons for Wilf. Swimming is an interesting one because, even though it's high-ranking on the faff front, I am convinced that such classes *do* deliver on what is promised in terms of helping the baby to grow into a toddler and then a child who is confident in the water. It makes sense to start them early and you almost have to look at it as an investment – you might not see an immediate return but you hope it's sensible speculation for later. I certainly had to keep telling myself that, when, after wrestling a four-month-old-baby Wilf into a neoprene wetsuit on top of *two* swim nappies (adhering to the 'doubling up' policy of the private pool, which is in place for obvious reasons), he proceeded to stare at me as though I were deranged for the duration of his half-hour session, even failing to crack a smile at the end, when I whizzed him around with one of those little fish-shaped mirrors, singing, 'Your lesson is over, we've had such fun! It's time to go home and tell everyone!'

However, I think our perseverance has paid off, as he's not even two and can already swim a hundred metres. Joking, of course, but he does now seem to enjoy the sessions and we get lots of splashing and laughter. As I only have one day off with just Wilf, I've found I look forward to the classes, too. He still seems to go a bit rogue when it comes to some of the more complex activities, such as a 'dolphin swim', where I sit him on the side of the pool, turn my back to him and then encourage him to put his arms around my neck so that I can swim off with him on my back. I'm pretty sure it should be instinctive for him to keep holding on and yet, every week, he simply lets go and launches himself into the water as I watch the other babies cling tightly to their mums and dads, gliding their way across the shallow end. That's just Wilf.

The one thing all the activities we've trialled have had in common is that they've *all* resulted in me looking and feeling like an idiot. I've always taken comfort in the fact that everyone feels a bit self-conscious, but even that's not strictly true as, every now and again, you'll encounter a parent who bloody loves every minute and performs 'Row, Row, Row Your Boat' as though it were an audition for *The Voice*.

Do I regret going along to any of these classes? No. I continue to hope that, one day, when my children become renowned for something in a professional capacity, I'll be able to look back and think, *It was those classes that did that.* Besides, they are a parenting rite of passage, an initiation, and if you've never stood in a circle of other parents looking like a twat, then you haven't earned your stripes.

C

# Comforters

When they were first born, I looked forward to my boys having a special bear or comforter. I'd observed other kids repeatedly clutching something dear to them and it just seemed like such a lovely thing for them to have. A cute teddy, a bunny rabbit, perhaps one of those blankies or muslins that end up dog-eared from years of chewing. Something they'd have a real attachment to, something that could calm them and offer a sense of security when they were feeling tired, sad or unsettled.

The problem with your child forming an attachment to something that will soothe them when they are feeling tired, sad or unsettled is that whatever they become attached to then becomes as much a part of your family as the child. You might think this sounds cute – it's what you hoped for, after all – but the cute factor soon wears off when you find yourselves turning the car around forty miles into a journey because you've forgotten Smelly Mummy Pig.

Honestly, I could write a whole book about the adventures of that bloody pig. I had assumed, somewhat naively, that I would be able to *choose* my boys' special bears, believing that whichever bears or toys I consistently gave to them when they were babies would be the ones they formed attachments to. Not so. Peter Rabbit with a tiny felt satchel, a classic Winnie the Pooh and a beautiful Jellycat frog are among the 'special toys' chosen by me that my children have rejected in favour of a blue bedtime bear wearing a nightcap (Henry's Best Friend) and Jude's Smelly Mummy Pig, also known as Stinky Mummy Pig and Pig-Pig. Wilf doesn't seem to have settled on a special bear or comforter yet, but I'd put money on it not being Little Nutbrown Hare from *Guess How Much I Love You*, who is still sitting patiently, waiting for his affection. With any luck, he won't become attached to chewing something that looks like a scrotum sack, which is exactly what an upside-down Mummy Pig without her dress resembles, as pointed out by my Facebook followers, who queried why I had given my son a pink ball-bag teddy to nibble on when I posted a picture of him in the Legoland queue.

Some of our most stressful parenting moments to date have involved the temporary loss or misplacement of Best Friend or Smelly Mummy Pig. I thought I had cheated the system early on by buying back-ups, but this plan backfired for two reasons. Firstly, I didn't rotate the back-up bear/pig with the original (apparently, if you do this early enough, they become interchangeable in terms of smell, touch and appearance). Instead, we ended up with a Back-up Best Friend who didn't have chewed paws and ears like the real Best Friend and a Back-up Smelly Mummy Pig who wasn't nearly smelly enough. Even a one-year-old knows that a 'magic spin in the washing machine' doesn't fix ears and paws. Secondly – and this was a massive fail we somehow managed to execute with both Best Friend and Smelly Mummy Pig – the boys found the back-ups. Henry went snooping and found Back-up Best Friend hidden in a box under our bed (it could have been worse, I suppose), and with Smelly Mummy Pig, one day I did what you must never do and allowed the original and the back-up to be in the same room at the same time. I'll never forget Jude's face when he looked from one to the other and declared, *'Two Smelly Mummy Pigs! Look, Mummy, there's two!'* For a short while afterwards he insisted on taking them both everywhere with him and I seriously contemplated buying two further back-ups so we'd also have a back-up for the back-up but, thankfully, the not-so-smelly one was dumped after a couple of weeks.

We now live in permanent fear of losing Best Friend and Smelly Mummy Pig, and have had far too many close shaves, including several instances when we've had to drive back to somewhere we've left them or ask the grandparents to turn around after they've dropped the boys home then driven off with Smelly Mummy Pig still in the boot. Nobody in the house can sleep if those cuddly toys are not in their rightful beds. Forgetting either of them when on the way to the airport is akin to forgetting passports – there can be no holiday without them.

Despite the added stress they've brought us – be careful what you wish for, and all that – there are times when having a special bear or comforter really has been cute. When looking for a photo of Jude to use for something the other day, I realised that his rancid-smelling pig is by his side in almost every one (luckily, with her dress on and the right way round in most of them). Similarly, Best Friend features in a lot of Henry's toddler pictures and, even at seven, he's keen to have him close by at night.

After Jude sniffed Smelly Mummy Pig's strange little stick foot so much it fell off, all eyes were on me to fix her and I realised then just how attached to her *I* am, too. I found myself speaking to her throughout the operation, reassuring her that, although I'm pretty useless with a needle and thread, I would get her through it because Jude needed her. We all needed her. Under the stress of the operation, it got me thinking that perhaps I'd been wrong to try and push a classier type of bear, more to my liking, on the boys. Maybe there is something even more special about a bear or a toy that you *don't* choose for your child – the underdog bear, the unexpected ugly pig, which, for whatever reason, they choose for themselves. Perhaps they choose each other.

Christ, we really are doomed if we lose them.

# Common Ground

Last summer, I got on a train from London back to Devon which was delayed by three quarters of an hour. By the time it was ready for passengers, those passengers (me included) were positively itching to get on board so we all did that kind of walk-run where you're clearly rushing but can't quite bring yourself to sprint along the platform. To add to the excitement, the air conditioning wasn't working and a last-minute change of train following technical problems with the original meant that the seat-reservation tickets hadn't been transferred to the corresponding carriages of this new train. This left everyone hot and flustered as we tried to navigate where best to park our bums.

I'd booked an off-peak return, which meant I didn't have a specific seat reservation but could sit anywhere that was free – the obvious problem being that *all* the seats now appeared to be free so people who had reserved a seat kept showing me their tickets before booting me out of my place while muttering, in that typically British way, 'Really sorry, I think you're in my seat.' Now, I appreciate that if you've booked a seat, you expect to sit in that seat, but these were slightly extenuating circumstances. The train wasn't overcrowded so there were plenty of seats to go round. If everyone had just sat down without worrying about which seat they were in, nobody would have needed to move. I was starting to get a bit irked by the sweaty Musical Chairs.

I don't know about you, but I can't relax until I've got myself 'settled' in my seat. I like to put my coat in the overhead rack, plug my phone charger into the nearest socket and place my water bottle and snacks on the little fold-out tray. When a fourth passenger stopped beside me in the aisle, looked at my seat number, then at her ticket, then again at my seat number, I sighed and said, 'You're going to tell me I'm in your seat, aren't you?', to which she flashed an apologetic smile and pointed to her ticket, which confirmed she was indeed booked to sit in Coach D, seat 33A. Which was absolutely fine, except she could have just taken a fucking seat anywhere else on the train (obviously, that's not what I said, I just picked up my things again and shifted over to the seats that were opposite hers).

By this point, I was hot and bothered and I found myself feeling annoyed that she was able to get nice and settled in her seat, something I was *still* unable to do, as there were stragglers getting on and I figured it would only be a matter of seconds before I'd have to move again. I knew I shouldn't but, as I sat in limbo with nothing better to do, I found myself silently forming judgements about who she was and what she was like. Her shoes and bag looked expensive and her phone was clean, which I know is a strange observation, but my phone is permanently snot-smeared and on the edge of ruin from being picked up, slobbered on then dropped from great heights by the kids. I guessed she was around my age, perhaps slightly older, and I imagined her going back to a clean and tidy house to snuggle up to her husband, who was probably some kind of highly paid creative type with trendy clothes and thick-rimmed glasses. Her spotless phone rang and she started talking quite sternly to someone she was obviously in charge of.

'I did ask that you send it to me in draft form first, Tim. Now there's an error and it looks unprofessional, which reflects badly on me, not you, as it's my project. I am paying you to help and it would have been less hassle if I'd just done it myself.' As she continued to 'hmmm' and tut at poor Tim, who I can only imagine was grovelling for whatever typo he'd allowed to slip through the net, another phone rang and she told Tim she had someone on the other line and that she would call him back. 'The other line' was a whole extra phone!

Now I was *really* intrigued (and finally starting to get myself settled, because the train was moving and nobody else had asked me to shift seats). As she pulled the other phone out of her bag I noticed it was much less pristine than the first and that she answered it in a much softer, less corporate tone – perhaps it was an affair phone?! She was talking more quietly, giggling, and I was 90 per cent sure I'd heard her say, 'You're such a big boy'

– but this seemed a bit much even for an affair phone conversation, given the proximity of other passengers. When we pulled in at Reading and the train noise calmed, I was able to properly overhear her conversation, and the penny finally dropped.

'Did you let Daddy give Duckie a wash? Is Daddy there? Can I speak to him? Yes, I love you too. Infinity love and beyond.'

It wasn't an affair phone, it was her *mum phone*. Equally as tatty as mine, she clearly kept it separate to the one she relied on for work (good idea, that; perhaps I should follow suit). Her other half might well be a trendy creative type, but it sounded as though he'd had his hands full tackling potty-training and that Duckie had been caught in the crossfire. She was eager to get home to her baby, in the same way I was eager to get home to mine.

'How old is he?' I asked her, remembering that I'd be getting home after the boys' bedtime due to the delay. Thinking about them made me miss them and I felt like I needed to talk about them.

'Two and a half.' She smiled, bringing up a picture on the mum-phone of a dark-haired toddler with dimples wearing a *PJ Masks* costume.

'Oooh, he's a Catboy fan, is he? I've got three boys and the middle one likes *PJ Masks*. His favourite is Gekko.'

And we were off. An in-depth chat about toddlers and potty-training and how we missed them when we weren't at home but also felt like we needed to work, for all sorts of complex reasons. If she made it back before 7 p.m. she'd be just in time for the bedtime story, but it was touch and go because the train had been so late.

She had a much fancier taste in bags and shoes than I did and, it turned out, a house with several acres of land and a twice-weekly cleaner, but we were united by our chat about the kids. Everything else seems so irrelevant – *is* irrelevant – when you realise you're both just missing the small people in your life.

Parenting is a common ground like no other, a real leveller, and the train chat reminded me of that. It also reminded me that I shouldn't make judgements about people just because they kick me out of my seat and dress to impress. She got off at Taunton, mouthing 'Bye' as she continued to bollock Tim, who was probably more likely to shit his pants than her toddler. Lessons had hopefully been learned, she told him. I smiled and kept my fingers crossed that she would make it back for bedtime.

# Conflicting Advice

'Don't despair if your baby will only nap on you, let her snuggle – the washing can wait!'

'Don't let her make a habit out of falling asleep on you. She needs to learn to sleep independently!'

'Feed on demand – she knows when she's hungry!'

'Get her into a feeding routine, or everyone's a bit fucked, really.'

'A dummy might help her to self-soothe and can actually reduce the risk of SIDS.'

'Avoid introducing a dummy, they're so bad for speech development.'

c

'Never use the Cry It Out method. Your baby will grow up emotionally damaged if left to cry!'

'Don't immediately pick up your baby when she cries. It'll become a bad habit.'

'Don't rush when it comes to potty-training, it's so much easier when *they're* ready.'

'They should be potty-trained by three. Anything longer than that is too long.'

'You should talk to your toddler on their level. Treat them as an equal – they'll respond more positively to gentle discipline.'

'If you don't assert your authority, they won't respect you.'

# Desperation

Google defines desperation as 'a state of despair, typically one which results in rash or extreme behaviour'. As a parent, desperation manifests itself in the following ways:

- *Taking a crying baby out for a drive in the car at midnight.*

- *Taking a crying baby out for a walk around the block in their pram at midnight.*

- *Pacing around the house, patting your baby's bum (imitating your heartbeat in the womb), while* 'sssshhhing' in their ear before eventually switching your pacing to a side-to-side bounce, a position you will remain in until it's time for the next feed and the cycle of doom starts again.

- Elevating the cot or Moses basket with books to help with colic, until your bookshelves are bare and the baby is effectively standing.

- Throwing money that you don't have at things that will 'fix' your baby. This is likely to include cranial osteopathy, where a very nice practitioner will tell you that your baby's neck and head are stressed following the birth and then proceed to place their hands very gently on his or her head and body. To you, this appears to be doing fuck all but, somehow, the baby falls asleep and, to be honest, you'll pay £35 for half an hour's peace. There'll always be someone who will tell you it made her baby worse and another who will link to articles declaring there is no evidence it works, but you won't care because you need hope in your life right now.

- Downloading white-noise playlists on Spotify as you've heard babies like the sound of the hair dryer.

- Setting up camp next to your child's bed on the floor 'just until they are asleep' and realising three years later that you never did make it back to your own bed.

- Going down on your knees, clasping your hands together and begging your child to stop crying/whingeing/hitting/biting/being a nightmare.

- Whispering with panic, 'Just pack it in and I'll buy you a treat,' when you're in a posh public place and everyone is judging your children and your parenting.

- *Taking the kids swimming even though you hate swimming, solely because it has, to date, been a reliable way of guaranteeing a toddler nap in the afternoon and you want nothing more than a lie-down yourself. On the drive home, you will open all the car windows and shout, 'Don't sleep yet! We're nearly home!' to avoid the nap occurring before you're able to take advantage of it.*

- *Lying to your children about what time it is. When they are old enough to tell the time, this progresses to changing the clocks outside of clock-changing season.*

- *Cutting food your children won't eat into fun shapes they still won't eat.*

- *Giving in and just letting them have whatever they bloody want. You're done.*

# Dishonesty

It's never OK to lie to your kids. Except when it is, because, let's face it, being 100 per cent truthful to children, particularly small ones, is virtually impossible. I mean, you probably *could* do it. With grit and determination, you could go all Jim Carrey in *Liar Liar* on them and answer with the full, unadulterated truth every time they ask a question, but you'd have to accept that you would be going against the long-established grain of what childhood looks, sounds and feels like.

It has only occurred to me since becoming a parent just how much of the magic of childhood is based on lies. There is a layer of fabrication around many of the big events – Christmas, Easter, tooth-losing. I can't bring myself to further elaborate on what I'm talking about here because a) children might pick this book up and read it, and who am I to ruin Christmas?

(though if they go on to read 'V is for Vagina' I fear Christmas will now be the least of their worries) and b) the lies have become so entrenched I think I may have started to believe them again – even though deep down I know it is me and James who will put all the effort in but it will be a jolly geriatric, a giant bunny or a fairy (who shadily pays more for enamel in posher postcodes), who will get all the credit.

I know what you're thinking, you're thinking, *Ah, but those are good lies*, and I'm not about to disagree with you. I'm certainly not going to propose that we broadcast *The Truth about Christmas* like a party political broadcast, just before the CBeebies *Bedtime Story*. I'm just saying that, if these are 'good fibs', then surely the precedent has been set for the use of other white lies in parenting? The next time someone says to me, 'You really shouldn't lie to your children,' as they have in several 'Hey, hun, not one to interfere but . . .' messages I've received, I will ask them whether *they* just came straight out and ruined everyone's Christmas right from the get-go? I thought as much, *hun*.

If bribery is the backbone of parenting, which it absolutely is in our house, then white lies are the supporting tendons. I appreciate this doesn't sound like a particularly virtuous parenting style, and I can't see the 'bribe and lie' approach having its own Facebook group any time soon in the same way that, say, gentle parenting does, but I think it's important to point out, in defence of dishonesty, that the white lies of parenthood almost always serve one of two primary functions and neither is in any way ill intentioned.

Firstly, there are the white lies you tell your children to protect their feelings. I always try to strike a healthy balance between being frank with the boys about the world they live in and wrapping them in cotton wool, plus ear defenders, but in practice, even when the aim has been to be transparent about something, there have been many times when their concerned faces have told me that I need to backtrack on the transparency front. We quite often have the *Six o'Clock News* on during the week, because I've turned into my own parents and find myself saying, 'Mummy just wants to catch the headlines!' However, even pre-watershed news and current affairs can be pretty distressing and sometimes I just don't have the heart to admit to the kids the reality of what's going on. I tend to give them the level of information I feel is right when they query what the newsreader is talking about. *They're talking about a plane that has crashed in the sea. They are searching for all the passengers.* With Henry, I would probably tell him that, sadly, as the hours pass, the chances of finding anyone alive gets less likely, but when Jude looked at me, aged four, and said, 'It's OK, because Fireman Sam has a rescue boat and can save them!', I couldn't bring myself to say, 'That's a lovely thought, darling, but they're probably all already dead,' so I said simply, 'You bet he will!' then turned over to *The Simpsons*. He will learn soon enough and, if it's my job as a parent to shield him from harm, then surely not harming his feelings is part of that. 'Protecting him from the truth' means I am indeed lying to him, but I think I can live with that over the alternative.

The other way in which dishonesty can serve you well as a parent is when you use it to your own advantage, for leverage or to help you out of a tricky spot. It's an integral part of the incentivisation game. Whether it's as brazen as 'Santa Cam' rigged up to a smoke alarm to send live feeds back to the North Pole or something more subtle – 'Oh no! Soft play is closed for cleaning today, darling, it's such a shame' – you are the grown-up and it's your prerogative to be creative with the truth.

Henry, if you are reading this (now that you can read), this book is all pretend and everything Mummy says at home is fact. Love you.

# Dressing a Baby

In the Beginning, this is one of the greatest joys. Baby clothes are ridiculously cute and, as you await your baby's arrival, there is so much satisfaction to be gained from folding and re-folding little vests and sleepsuits as you deliberate over which ones should make the Hospital Bag cut. I can still remember with fondness the vests and sleepsuits we chose for all three of our boys. It makes me feel all warm and fuzzy inside.

When they are first born, it's something of a challenge to get said garments *on* the baby, mostly because you're worried you are going to damage him or her in the process. It can be tricky to get all the tiny fingers through to the end of the sleeves without bending one the wrong way (always the thumb), and God, why are their head and neck so floppy? Surely that's going to be a problem? However, you soon find your way and the dressing of your baby becomes quite a nice thing to do. Finally, you get to showcase all the cute stuff you've been stockpiling in drawers, though it's never long before you realise that buying anything resembling a proper outfit for babies, i.e. dungarees, chinos, anything with buttons, is a total waste of time and money that should be reserved solely for special occasions (and even then, nobody asks the baby to leave for not adhering to the dress code; just stick them in a onesie).

As your baby gets older and more mobile, the fun of getting them dressed diminishes. Trying to do the poppers up on the Babygro of a baby who can kick and crawl is a full-body work-out. This is when baby jogging bottoms come in handy or, if you're slovenly, like we are, you might find you do up a token few Babygro poppers, wonkily, and leave the rest open. He's only going in the pram, what does it matter?

# Dressing a Toddler

'Come here a second, pickle, I've just got to put some clothes on you.'

Repeat x 100.

Toddler remains naked.


# Dressing Yourself

You can forget that. Throw on whatever you find from the floordrobe before spraying some dry shampoo on your fringe. Good to go.

# Early

5 a.m. is early.

6 a.m. is borderline early but acceptable as a time to get up.

7 a.m. is not early.

7.30 a.m. is a lie-in!

8 a.m. means you must have given your kids an iPad with 100 per cent battery and told them not to bother you until it runs out of charge.

9 a.m. is practically lunchtime.

(4 a.m., or anything starting with a 4, even if it's 04.59, is still the middle of the night.)

# Emotional

There are a great many parenting feelings I had underestimated. Probably all of them, if truth be told. It's as though the moment I started cooking our first small human, someone extracted all my emotional responses, injected them with steroids and then reinjected the beefed-up version when I wasn't looking.

'It's just your hormones,' I have been told many times, and there have been a few occasions when this has been the case. Soupgate was one such example, when, at eight months pregnant (third time around) I decided to make some tomato soup as a 'snacky tea', albeit one with a slightly higher nutritional value than my usual effort. As a decidedly non-cooky person, I was quite pleased with how it turned out – a little thick but packed full of veggies; I'd even added some fresh basil, so I was feeling very *MasterChef*.

'Come and get it, boys!' I said, optimistic that everyone would enjoy my wholesome offering.

Henry had been the first to crack. 'I don't like it,' he said with a grimace. As this wasn't unusual, I stayed positive, encouraging him to dip his bread in instead.

Then came Jude. 'Eurrrghhh, it's disgusting! IT'S ALL OVER MY BREAD, MY BREAD IS DIRTY!'

Throughout their display of dissatisfaction, James was unusually quiet and I noticed he was taking very small spoonfuls of soup and sipping it gingerly. He caught my gaze before admitting, 'I have to be honest, babe, I'm not that keen either.'

Well, that was it. I burst into tears at the table – full-on sobs – while the three men in my life stared at me with their soup spoons suspended in mid-air, mouths wide open, unsure of what to do. James left his chair and came around to comfort me, telling me that he was sure it was lovely but that he just wasn't 'a big tomato soup fan'. The kids stared some more. Jude asked tentatively if he could have a yoghurt, then wiped his tongue on his sleeve to get rid of the yucky soup taste, before finally Henry said, 'I like the one in the tin.' So that was that. I made a point of finishing my bowl through my tears, vowing to 'never bloody bother' again.

Other hormone-induced incidents include having a meltdown over a dirty dishcloth (it was during peak nesting season) and crying because I saw a lone duck on the River Exe that didn't have any friends. Once, as a new mum, I was watching one of those animal-rescue programmes and I felt my boobs let-down at the sight of kittens being born. A powerful force indeed, those pesky chemical messengers.

However, I am certain that my amplified emotional state post-children cannot solely be blamed on hormones. Seven years in to this crazy adventure, I am at least 50 per cent more emotional than I was pre-kids and I'd say it's looking like a pretty permanent upscale on the feelings front. It's not always a bad thing, of course, and there is certainly no shame attached to feeling all the feels, but I do at times still find myself bowled over by their intensity.

I worry a lot more. I cry a lot more. I shout a lot more. I feel that bubbling, irritated annoyance (where you resort to practising labour breathing to avoid blowing your fuse) a lot more. But I also smile a lot more. I laugh a lot more. The warm and fuzzy feelings are so much warmer and so much fuzzier. Every year, at Henry's Nativity, I only need to clock eyes on the little shepherds walking into the hall with tea towels on their heads and I'm sobbing.

It's a bit unsettling to know that I no longer have control over my emotions in the same way that I perhaps once did, but I'm starting to embrace the streaming eyes and blotchy face and accept that they're always going to happen, because I am just so bloody proud of my kids. Never has there been a cuter Wise Man.

I'm crying again. FFS.

# Equal Treatment

No matter how good your intentions are, 'We'll treat them both the same' is an impossible promise to make to yourselves. It just isn't viable to give your second (or third, or fourth) child the same level of undivided attention that you gave your first child because, just by having those subsequent children, you *are forced to* divide your attention. 'Undivided' no longer exists. As you stumble through the first months of parenting a new baby for the second time, you are probably also (depending on the age gap) having to look after a toddler, or do the school-run, or, if you've joined the 'two under two' club, take care of another baby.

The opportunities to gaze lovingly at the newest addition are lessened as you find yourself running around the living room encouraging your firstborn to poo on the potty and not in the lid of the Duplo tub, like last time. You'll be determined to capture all of your second baby's milestones in the same way you lovingly documented your first baby's 'firsts', but when there is a three-year-old having an ear-splitting tantrum because you're all out of Babybels or a six-year-old needing help with phonics homework, it's quite easy to miss the first crawl or the first coherent babble of your youngest.

The truth is, Jude wasn't treated the same as his big brother. He's had less fuss, fewer photos and a far greater number of occasions when he's been left to play independently because we've been tied up with something else. Probably not by coincidence, he is happy to entertain himself and far less demanding of our attention, unlike Henry, who had our full attentiveness for nearly three years and, at seven, still protests he is 'really bored' when left to his own devices for five seconds.

I know what you're thinking. What on earth does this mean for our *third* child? By the above depleting-attention logic, poor Wilf must surely be clothed in rags, playing on his own and eating his dinners out of the bin. Well, it's not quite *that* bad, but I would be lying if I said he was treated equally to Jude and, if you compare his treatment to that of his eldest brother as a baby, you'd be forgiven for thinking they must have different parents. It took a year for a photo of Wilf to grace the walls of our house. I have never once made him a baby purée from scratch, like I did with Henry and, whereas Jude at least enjoyed the baby jars warmed up and decanted into colourful bowls, Wilf has learned to slurp an Ella's Kitchen Chick-Chick Chicken Casserole straight from the pouch, cold, when in his stroller. This is not something I'm proud of.

He doesn't have a bedtime story every night, nor do we massage his little arms and legs with olive oil after a bath. All TV guidelines (see Screen time) went out of the window when we realised putting 'Baby Shark (Doo Doo Doo Doo Doo Doo)' on the iPad meant he would stop crying long enough for us to wrestle him into a clean nappy. 'Yeah, he'll be all right' is our default answer to every question asking if he should really be allowed to do or eat something.

Despite all of this, Wilf and Jude have something Henry didn't have, and that's the company of people their own size. Wilf may at times look a bit dishevelled and I may have turned a blind eye when he was eating a three-day-old floor Cheerio, but he has two big brothers who look out for him, who shout, 'Mum, Wilf's trying to lick the telly!' and who try to make him laugh when they can see that I am struggling. There are times when he has the most attention, accumulatively. It's just never undivided. I'm hoping that, because he's never known what it feels like to be our one and only, it's not something he can 'miss'. In time, he'll benefit from having two older brothers who'll have pushed the boundaries of adolescence (and what they can get away with) before he has to, and whose Lynx he can pinch.

# Exercise

'But exercise is so good for you!' exclaimed a friend of mine who was having a hard time trying to understand why I wasn't doing anything active in my spare time. It was quite simple, I told her. I no longer had 'spare time'. Plus, running around after two kids (this was pre baby number three) was quite enough physical activity, thank you very much. I hated the thought of exercise, I hated the smug people who did lots of exercise and I hated being made to feel guilty for not doing any exercise. Any reference I made to exercise on social media was along the lines of, 'If you see me running, there must be something chasing me LOLZ #cantrunwontrun.'

Over time, it was almost as though the less exercise I did, the greater number of excuses I made for why I wasn't doing any. I think I genuinely believed that there were obstacles preventing me from working up any kind of sweat. *Exercise isn't for me because I don't have a personal trainer and membership to one of those posh health clubs with a crèche and all the gym/sauna/steam room trimmings. I can't exercise because I have work to do, and when I'm not working I have kids to look after – I hardly have the luxury of time to get myself in shape!*

This remained my mind-set for the best part of five years, and it's only been in the last year, after joining a 'couch to 5k' running group at Henry's school, that, I have realised my friend was right. Exercise *is* good for me, and I'm not just talking about my body, though it's good for that, too. I mean it's good

E

for my mental health, which has improved dramatically since I joined the group.

Once a week, after school drop-off, I go for a run with some other mums. I very nearly backed out at the last minute because I didn't know any of them and had convinced myself that they would all be fitter and healthier than me, but forcing myself to go with them that first week is one of the best decisions I have ever made. Our group often has to walk because the hills are too hilly and we're all a bit knackered. Sometimes, one of us is hungover. At least one member of the group is struggling to give up smoking, we constantly talk about food and, one time, we ate bacon sandwiches instead of going running – so we're not exactly an elite running clique.

I doubt I'll ever be someone who 'smashes out a 10k' or 'chases the gains', but I've realised it's not an all-or-nothing thing. I *need* that forty-five-minute blowout. Even if I do nothing else in terms of physical activity for the rest of the week, when running-club morning rolls around I make sure I go. I run, sweat, walk if I have to and, bloody Nora, I feel better for it afterwards.

I am including this entry just in case there is someone reading this book who thinks, *That's easy for you to say, but I don't do exercise*, because I know what that feeling is like. I'm still not exercise's biggest fan, but that little jog once a week has made me feel happier, less tired and less likely to want to throw something at other members of my family, and all without having to pay a penny for some swanky membership. Doing something as a group has also been a revelation – I've made friends, found common ground and it's so much more fun than I ever thought exercise could be. If you can steal an hour in your week, half an hour even, to do something active – whatever that may be – please don't assume like I did for so long that exercise was for the other sorts of mums. Anyone can do it. Besides, three quarters of an hour jogging or swimming or yoga-ing equates to a guilt-free takeaway and a bottle of wine. Fact.*

. . . . . . . . . . . . .

* Possibly not a fact. I burned so few calories on one of our feeblest jog/ walks my running app told me I'd earned the equivalent of a small banana.

# Feeding

I was on the fence for a long time about whether I should include anything about feeding in this book, which is all kinds of crazy when you think about how much time a baby spends feeding and, by default, how much time you spend feeding them. My hesitation came about because I'm just really bloody tired of being attacked every time I write anything about how I have fed *my* babies (never a commentary on how anybody else has fed theirs) and this has put me right off saying anything at all. Which I realised is enough ammo for a little section of its own.

Luckily, this isn't like Facebook or Instagram, where people can instantly comment on my post, though if somebody really wants to write me a letter about how disappointed they are in my feeding commentary (this has happened before), they can do so and I'll be ready for it. Best address is The Unmumsy Mum, PO Box Couldn't Give a Shit.

If you're thinking 'attacked' sounds a bit dramatic, below is a selection of just some of the messages I have received following posts about feeding.

When I was breastfeeding:

> *Hooray for you, you're breastfeeding. Is it really necessary to have your tits out on Instagram Stories?*
>
> *I used to love following you on here, but no one cares about how your baby is 'latching on' or your milk 'let-downs'. It's so dull.*

When I wasn't:

> *Your [sic] basically saying that you couldn't be bothered to keep breastfeeding so your [sic] sticking him on the bottle. Not a great message, is it? Next thing, you'll probably do an advert for formula.*
>
> *I feel sad for Wilf that you don't care about doing what's best for him. Yes, it can be hard, but that's not enough of a reason to throw the towel in. Lazy parenting.*

The last one was the final straw on a day when I was highly emotional anyway, and left me in floods of tears. My hormones were all over the place and I was, without exaggeration, devastated that our breastfeeding journey had come to an end, a decision I hadn't taken lightly but knew was the right one for us as a family after Wilf's tongue-tie and subsequent feeding and weight issues had left me feeling mentally very low. I know, I know. I'm justifying myself. I shouldn't feel the need to explain myself to anyone but, considering the backlash any kind of feeding statement attracts, it's hardly surprising that I struggle to say, 'I stopped breastfeeding him at seven weeks,' without fleshing it out with excuses to avoid further judgement.

The craziest thing about the abuse I have received online from 'both sides', aside from the fact that there really are people who identify with a 'side', is that I have only ever shared what has been true for us. I bigged up breastfeeding when it was going well, which was apparently wrong because it made me look smug and rubbed it in the faces of mums who couldn't breastfeed. When I was honest about our decision to switch to the bottle, that was also wrong because I was encouraging mums to not bother breastfeeding. I literally could not win. And let's not forget the time I included the words 'fed is best' in a blog post and the Internet reacted like I'd advocated feeding the baby heroin. The thing is, I never said that I believed fed was best for the *baby* but, surely, when considering the bigger picture of what's 'best', it's not too radical a concept to take into account what's best for mum too?

So I'm not going to apologise for saying that Wilf was doing well on formula, because he was, and I'm not going to apologise for talking about enjoying the time I'd spent breastfeeding the bigger boys, because I did. So there. That feels better.

# Fish Fingers

Once upon a time, a journalist called Anna May Mangan wrote an article for the *Mail Online* referencing me and a number of other bloggers under the following headline: *Feeding their toddlers frozen fish fingers, swigging gin from baby cups and potty-mouthed ranting about their kids online: Why ARE so many women boasting they're slummy mummies?*

If you missed it, this is what I wrote back (and we've been pen pals* ever since).

Dear Anna May Mangan,

I would usually start a letter with some textbook niceties, perhaps, 'I hope this finds you well,' or something about the weather, but I am just about to stick some fish fingers in the oven and crack open another bottle of Sauv Blanc, so I'll cut to the chase.

When I woke up this morning I discovered I had an unusually high number of social media notifications, alongside several 'Have you seen the *Mail Online* yet?' messages. A couple of years ago, this early-morning flurry of online activity would almost certainly have thrown me into a sicky panic, but this morning there was no such fear as I clicked through to your article. I already knew what it would say. In fact, if I had put money on it, I would have been on the lookout for a five-point attack:

Something about being slummy. Check.
Something about swearing. Check.
Something about alcohol. Check.
Something about fish fingers. Check.
An overriding message about how mums should cherish every single moment. Check.

· · · · · · · · · · · · ·

* Never heard from her again.

I do think it's a bit of a shame that you felt the need to attack a group of mum bloggers and authors, but I completely understand why you did. We are terrible parents, or at the very least we are all masquerading as terrible parents simply for likes and shares. That's not how us mums should behave, I can see that now. It would be so much healthier for the maternal nation if we all swept our bad days under the carpet. I promise I will try harder.

The thing is, if you had taken the time to properly read any of my stuff, you would have come across the many heartfelt chapters I've dedicated to my boys, and indeed my own mother, who died of cancer when I was young. You would have known that I regularly beat myself up for not cherishing every sodding second but that, on balance, I have decided that sharing the good, the bad and the ugly is more important. Potty-training is ugly. Fact.

You say that you 'appreciate how this "honesty" could make new mums feel less isolated and more reassured', but I couldn't help but mutter 'Bullshit' when I read that token paragraph, particularly noting that you also say, 'These arrogant women shouldn't forget that, as well as being hard, a new baby is a gift.'

That was the point at which I knew I had to say something. For all the mums out there who, like me (and the others you reference in your article – all pals of mine, actually; we like to have Slummy Mummy Squad meetings) might read your bile and feel bad for having the odd moan.

Admitting to serving up beige frozen goods ('freezer tapas', we like to call it; we're very middle class), confessing to the odd hangover and occasionally ranting about the inability to go to the toilet without a small person trying to unwrap our sanitary items is not boasting, Anna. It's just real life. Whether or not you choose to believe that what we are documenting is, in fact, our real lives is not really any concern of mine. I shan't lose any sleep over a lack of endorsement from the *Mail*. The point of this post is simply to say *Shame on you* for failing to recognise the wider importance of this so called 'slummy mummy movement'.

If taking snaps of fish fingers, cursing the bastard stray Lego impaling my feet in the middle of the night and offering a virtual hug to mums who are having a shitty day is wrong, then shoot me down, I don't want to be right.

I would like to conclude by saying a massive thank you for sending an extra thousand or so followers my way just this morning and pushing both my books back up the chart. (I'm guessing that probably wasn't your intention, but I am ever so grateful; thank you.) I couldn't help but think your mention of our bestselling books smacked of jealousy, which I can't for the life of me understand, when your own parenting manual, *The Pushy Mother's Guide*, sounds like an absolute classic.

Have a lovely day. I know I will.

Yours sincerely,

Sarah Turner
A boastful slummy mummy from Devon

F

# Fuck-it Bucket

Some parenting days seem destined to go wrong. Days when your patience is tested beyond belief and you're quite tempted to ask for your money back, or at the very least negotiate an exchange for a child who doesn't smirk and/or fart in your face when you're trying to talk to them about respect. Step forward the fuck-it bucket (FIB): a conceptual final resting place for the most frustrating of days, the ones that have wound up being an absolute disaster.

A FIB day might have its roots in the mother of all tantrums, or it might develop following a slow but steady build-up of whingeing over several hours which has culminated in a meltdown over a milkshake being too milky or a vocalised injustice that it's June and not Christmas. Such days will almost always involve the refusal to put shoes on, a spike in your blood pressure, at least one person crying and empty threats about confiscating something or cancelling a party. Whatever you had planned for dinner will be sacked off in favour of something convenient with a dubious percentage of real meat content.

The thing is, nobody wakes up in the morning, contemplates what to do with the day then settles on a nice afternoon of standing at the bottom of the stairs shouting, 'We do not shout!' I am quite often mortified by the sound of my own mum-voice, which is much less like the calm and patient Mary Poppins tone I'd always imagined I'd possess and more like the ear-piercing screech of Bianca off EastEnders when she got mad at Riccckkyyyy. I hate myself when Shouty Mum comes out to play, but there is often a very good reason why she shows up.

If you ever find you're nearing the end of a day where you've lost your shit, or the kids have lost the plot, make use of the

FIB to draw a mental line under whatever catastrophe has unfolded. I find it helpful to imagine a bin or a basket somewhere, so I can picture myself physically offloading my Day of Doom after I've finally got the little terrors to sleep. I didn't start employing the FIB strategy until after we'd had our second baby and I've definitely noticed a welcome decline in the amount I beat myself up after a disastrous day. It's the parenting equivalent of handing yourself a Get Out of Jail Free card, a way of unburdening yourself of the usual overanalysis so you don't sit and stew on your bad day when you could be unwinding in front of the telly. Wipe the slate clean and start again in the morning. Tomorrow is a new day.

# Fussy Eaters

I watched a programme about fussy-eating kids when I was pregnant for the second time. Henry, who was two and a half, had become a terribly picky eater. The programme confirmed that this was, of course, all my fault. Kids are only fussy if you allow them to be fussy. Start them off on the right track, with *positive habits*, and they won't develop such precious tendencies in the first place. I was greatly looking forward to hearing more about what the children of the fussy-eating expert ate at home – perhaps they started the day with some pumpernickel toast and boysenberry jam – but alas, it turned out she didn't have children of her own. (Though if she did, they wouldn't be fussy, because of the positive habits.)

For a short while, Henry's love of bland foods and distrust of vegetables worried me. I allowed myself to be sucked into forum threads and parenting manuals, looking for ways to fix him. The problem with being the firstborn is that you're

treated like a living experiment – your parents haven't done this before, they don't know when they should worry or when they should just chill out a bit. It really is the blind leading the blind and that is why, when it came to Henry's fussy eating, we tried pretty much everything. Firstly, we tried slowly introducing different textures, starting with purées and blended vegetables (just like he'd had as a baby) and gradually working up to a lumpier, bittier texture. That didn't work because he still didn't trust the colour of the meat or vegetables, even when blended. We tried dividing up the different foods on his plate into their own little sections, as something I'd read suggested it wasn't the individual foods themselves that children have an issue with but the mix of them all together. Unsurprisingly, that didn't work either – he simply ate whatever was beige, plain and bland – chips, bread, pasta, Yorkshire puddings – and left all the other sections untouched. We tried the 'like it or lump it' approach, where of course he lumped it, happier to go on hunger strike than entertain the idea of eating a tomato; followed by the incentivising angle – 'If you eat what's on your plate, you can have a chocolate mousse' – which had slightly more success, but by the end of a fraught mealtime we'd find ourselves on our knees begging him just to lick the sweet potato, touch it even, and we'd give him a KitKat.

It was after I got chatting to an elderly woman at the doctor's that I decided I would stop worrying. I was telling her all about our feeding woes and she was listening sympathetically and nodding, before she said, 'I wouldn't fret quite so much, dear. It's unlikely that he'll grow up to only eat plain pasta. At some point, he'll probably eat a carrot and quite like it. Then, one day, he'll order seafood in a fancy restaurant and you'll laugh about all this.' She was right. I knew she was right. It's rare to come across an adult who orders a roast dinner then only eats the 'safe' potatoes that haven't been 'ruined' by the gravy. From that moment, I stopped having tactics at teatime. I put food on his plate, encouraged him to eat it and sometimes, if he really hated it, I gave him a slice of bread and butter instead, which Mrs Fussy Eating Expert would undoubtedly have scowled at.

If adopting a more relaxed and liberal approach to his eating was the experiment, it has paid off. At seven, he is no longer fussy. He is still suspicious of sauces with 'bits' in, dislikes sweet potatoes, and if you serve up a casserole he may crumple to the ground, but those things aside, he eats well. He likes olives! He'll eat sprouts. He has been known to ask his grandad for a little packet of sushi rather than a sandwich in M&S and he'll polish off pretty much whatever is on the menu for school dinners. Had we kept on and on at him with our desperate meal coaching, with every dinnertime becoming a battle where we kept tabs on whether he had swallowed the pea he was eating, rather than spending time chatting to each other, I do wonder if we might have done more harm than good.

When Jude came along, we did attempt to rectify some of the 'mistakes' we'd apparently made with baby Henry by introducing different textures sooner, mixing in some baby-led weaning and generally encouraging a love of a greater variety of foods from a younger age, and guess what? He, too, was fussy during the toddler years, with a dislike of everything that wasn't a 'snacky tea' (chicken dippers, chips, *no* beans). It's only now, at four, that he's started to eat proper grub, and even then it's hit and miss (except when he's at nursery, when he'll happily tuck in to Thai red curry then ask for seconds, the little sod).

If you're currently battling with a fussy eater, please know that a child who only eats plain, beige carbs can turn into a child who'll eat fish pie, without picking out the fish, in just a few years. As that wise woman at the doctor's said, I wouldn't fret quite so much, dear.

# Gender

People, particularly strangers, will obsess over the gender of your child right from the start of your pregnancy. They will 'know' what you are having. They can 'just tell'. I once met a man in Wilko who said, with a wink, 'That's a little girl in there. One hundred per cent. I'm never wrong on these!' as though he were forecasting the weather. I didn't have the heart to tell him I sincerely hoped he was wrong, being as I'd seen a willy and balls at the scan the week before.

If you already have one child, assumptions are made regarding gender or, more specifically, your *preference* towards gender from the moment you announce a subsequent

69

pregnancy. The assumption is always that you want whatever flavour you haven't already got. This is exceptionally
annoying, particularly when you know you're expecting Boy
Number Three and people look at you like you've just told
them your dog has died. Often this is accompanied by a
slight head tilt or one of those tuts people do to express that
something is a shame, followed by a quick attempt to make
you feel better, even though you're feeling perfectly fine,
thank you very much.

'As long as they're healthy, eh? And you'll be able to pass
down all the clothes, so that's handy!'

'Boys love their mums, though, don't they? That's a bonus.'

'Probably easier in many ways – you already know what
you're doing!'

Sometimes they'll tell you a story you haven't got time for
about their neighbour's sister Beryl who had eleven girls before
she had a boy – 'Eleven girls, mind!' – or say something that's
actually pretty offensive, such as, 'There's always next time' or
'Fourth time lucky, then!' as though you've taken a coin to three
scratch cards and found no winners so far.

You should know, however, that although it's OK for *strangers*
to feel disappointed on your behalf about the gender of your
unborn child, it's not OK for you to express any such disappointment. I was very open about feeling sad that we weren't
having a girl the second time around (*not* disappointment that
we were having another boy, just disappointment that I'd never
have a daughter) and, even though I received hundreds of stories in return from parents who have found themselves in the
same boat, the general consensus seems to be that you must
never say it out loud. Unfortunately, I'd blogged about it and
had it immortalised in book form by then. Oops.

I've observed that there tends to be a standard script for
whatever gender dynamic you find yourself blessed with.

# G

If you have two (or more) girls, sympathies will be offered to the dad, who will be preposterously outnumbered for the rest of his life. Jokes will be made about him having to give up his dreams of playing football with the boys, even if he's never been interested in sport, because that's what all dads dream about doing and everyone knows girls can't play football.

The same can be said for mums and boys. She will be told she can borrow a niece to take shopping, or offered condolences for the number of Sundays she will spend on the edge of a pitch watching yep, you guessed it, football! Because that's what all boys like doing, and everyone knows mums hate football.

If you have one of each, by strangers' standards you have hit the jackpot. Consequently, if you announce that you are having a third child, people will assume this must have been an accident. If you weren't trying for either a boy or a girl, what the hell *were* you trying for?! Simply wanting another child doesn't seem to be reason enough.

I should point out here that, even though my eyes might roll right back into my head when confronted with gender stereotypes, our boys are, thus far, a living and breathing gender stereotype, and sometimes this pains me, particularly as I did all the things I could to avoid the 'boys will be boys' path. I shut them down if ever they said, 'Those toys are for girls' or commented on something being 'too girly' because it was pink. I bought them dollies with prams, resulting in Jude's brief but nevertheless adorable love affair with Baby Richard. I encouraged them to dance and do gymnastics, alongside going to Rugby Tots. We played with Sylvanian Families houses and acted out scenes from *Frozen*. If they wanted to wear some of Mummy's make-up, they wore some of Mummy's make-up. Gender, I told James, particularly when it came to kids' toys and games, was a social construct.

We then watched as Baby Richard was cruelly discarded in favour of Monster Trucks, as the boys' dancing turned into amateur attempts at martial arts (on each other) and as Henry declared that he didn't really play with the girls at his school because they were doing 'girl stuff'. For the majority of 2017 and 2018, all they talked about was wrestling, and my joy at finding Jude playing happily with his dolls' house was cut short when I realised he was acting out putting The Undertaker and Stone Cold Steve Austin to bed.

I think, sometimes, as much as it pains me to say it, boys really will be boys.

# Good Enough

'What's the one piece of parenting advice you would give a new mum or mum-to-be?' I've lost count of the number of times I have been asked this question, and I have always given subtle variations of the same answer. Be kinder to yourself, don't compare yourself to others, don't assume that what you see on somebody else's social media is their reality, never be afraid to ask for help, cut yourself some slack. I wholeheartedly believe in all those things, too, but if I had to offer just *one* piece of advice, it would be this: lower the bar.

I know I run the risk of sounding like a negative Nancy by putting forward bar-lowering as my one parenting pearl of wisdom. I know, too, that there will be many pregnant mums living in a bubble of optimism who neither want nor need a frazzled mum-of-three advising them to reduce their parenting standards before they've even started. Presumably, lowering the bar means lowering the quality of your parenting, and that can never be a good thing. Can it?

Well, I believe it can. I think new parents should actively seek to lower their expectations of their own parenting, and that's not because I'm endorsing carelessness or ineptitude but simply because I'm convinced that the expectations we set for ourselves at the outset of our parenting adventures are too bloody high. The bar is too high. What then follows is the inevitable but nevertheless crushing realisation that we have failed to achieve the level of parenting we'd planned/hoped/expected, even though the level we *have* achieved is ample.

I'm not a big fan of those inspirational quotes you see plastered all over social media – you know the ones, something about living every day as if it's your last, dancing in the rain and being the change you want to see ... yadda yadda yadda – but there was a quote doing the rounds on Instagram recently that really struck a chord with me. It said: *You can do anything but not everything.*

Never has that been truer than in the context of parenting. So many of us start out with an unrealistic vision of what we'll be like as parents, often informed by the images we've been fed online and in print of well-dressed mums with perfectly behaved children who always smile and never shout, living in beautifully decorated houses. Even if we know deep down that those images are not the full story, if that's all we see, it's hardly surprising that after a while we start to internalise them. The problem is, the bar has then been set precariously high and it's not even a real bar!

How much more enjoyable would it be if we just accepted that there will be many occasions in our parenting lives when something has to give, and that unless we want that something to be our mental health, lowering the bar more generally is a good place to start? Set the bar to line up with what *you* think is important – your own priorities, not a pie-in-the-sky version of parenting cooked up from the selectively edited bumf that tells you you'll never be good enough. If you want to make all your baby food from scratch, do. If you find you can't relax until the dishes have been put away and the living room has been hoovered, put the dishes away and hoover. But don't for one moment assume that you are failing if you find yourself feeding a baby from jars and pouches in a kitchen that looks like it's been hit by an earthquake. For every mum who disinfects the worktops thrice daily, there's a mum who's just discovered a three-week-old ham sandwich under the sofa cushions. For every mum whose toddler eagerly polishes off organic home-made lunches, there's a mum who considers it a win if her toddler eats anything that doesn't come out of a packet. For every mum who is shit hot at making fancy-dress costumes, there is a mum who always forgets it's Halloween and ends up raiding the first-aid kit for bandages in a desperate attempt at a 'Scary Mummy' costume which looks a bit shit because there's only enough bandage to wrap around the head.

Don't try to do everything. Don't put pressure on yourself to do something that you didn't even know was A Thing until Jenny on Mumsnet made you feel guilty about not doing it.

The truth is, however hard you try, you could always be doing more. The question is, do you need to? Sometimes 'good enough' really is enough. Lower that bar.

# Google

Just a few of the many obscure but at the time perfectly reasonable pregnancy and parenting-related quandaries I have put to the fount of all knowledge that is Google.

# G

Baby won't sleep

Baby won't latch on

Best cabbage for sore boobs

Bibs with arms

Can babies eat cheese?

Excessive farting in pregnancy

Green poo

Have I got a prolapse?

Postpartum hair loss

Signs of tongue-tie

Toddler won't nap

Toddler won't eat

Toddler won't poo

Toddler won't walk on reins

Vasectomies, Devon

# Grandparents

I feel like I should write an 'Ode to Grandparents', something meaningful to reflect their value. Perhaps a haiku?

*Givers of sweet treats*
*Good Heavens! Hasn't he grown?*
*Here, have a Freddo.*

In all seriousness, grandparents deserve a shout-out. I know, of course, that not everyone has the luxury of grandparents who live nearby. I know, too, that even if they do live nearby, it doesn't always mean those grandparents are willing or able to help out, and that sometimes relationships between generations are tense or have broken down completely. There will also be many mums and dads out there whose own mums and/or dads are no longer alive – this one I, sadly, have experience of first hand because my boys have only ever 'met' their Nanny

Debbie through photographs. However, they are *incredibly* fortunate to have (and we are incredibly fortunate that they have!) a Nanny and Grandad in James's mum and dad and a Grandad Shep and Granny in my dad and step-mum, all of whom live within an hour's drive and who have been hugely important in their lives so far.

So important, in fact, that our kids prefer their grandparents to us, their parents. I don't mean that in a jokey way, I mean it quite literally. Given the choice, I have no doubt that our children would opt to live with *our* parents. Alas, at the time of writing, I haven't managed to persuade either set of grandparents to sign the necessary forms.

We benefit from what I think is the optimum geographical distance of close-but-not-too-close between our house and their houses. You may think it's scandalous to suggest grandparents could ever be 'too close' but, in practical terms, as well as being too far away to just pop in unannounced (just not a fan of pop-ins; no offence, Dad), a little bit (but not a lot) of distance means they spend quality time with the boys when they do come up, which is usually once a week. James and I have had varying work patterns between us since the boys came along, a mix of full time, part time and no time, and the boys' grandparents have done – and continue to do – so much for us to help with childcare. It's not something we take for granted and we hope they know they don't *have* to do it – we'd just move to France if the childcare dried up (joking – kind of. I do quite fancy Nice).

There's so much to love about grandparents. If you gloss over their determination to rot their grandkids' teeth with 'the occasional little treats' that are neither little nor occasional, they are a godsend. I can count on one hand the number of nights away from the kids James and I have had (together) since Henry arrived on the scene in 2012, but those nights have been glorious and all have been made possible by grandparent babysitting favours. They have also stepped in on numerous occasions when they sensed we were about to implode under the pressure of renovating a house with three children at large and will probably never know how much that respite was appreciated.

Grandparents, we love and salute you.

PS Do you fancy having the boys for a sleepover next weekend?

# Guilt

One Friday afternoon after school last year I bundled a three-month-old Wilf into his pram, instructed Henry to put his school shoes and coat back on and pushed us all out the door to pick up Jude from nursery. It's only a short walk to nursery but we are often running late, which leaves me feeling flustered, a feeling that's not aided by the incessant *Minecraft* chat from Henry, who doesn't pause for breath as he tells me something 'really interesting' about Endermen and Nether Portals. Despite the rush of a school run closely followed by a nursery run, I like Fridays. After we've collected Jude, we pop into the little shop down the road, where I let the boys choose a packet of sweets each, and then we all return home, the walk back marking the start of the weekend.

On the Friday in question, however, my chipper mood evaporated the moment I asked Jude's key worker, as I always do, if he'd had a good day. Yes, she told me, he'd had a lovely day. He'd played happily in the garden with the other children and then he'd helped to make scones for the party tea.

*Scones for the party tea.*

Momentary confusion before the penny dropped.

## G

Scones for the 'Mother's Day Treat' party tea. Scones for the Mother's Day Treat party tea I'd RSVP'd 'Yes' to. Scones for the Mother's Day Treat party tea I'd written in my diary and yet somehow had completely forgotten about. I'd missed it. *Shit.*

'Ah yes, the party tea!' I responded, with my best 'I hadn't forgotten' face. 'I was really hoping to make it, but something came up. Did you have fun, pickle?' I smiled but, inside, as Jude made his way over to me, my heart was breaking as I pictured him looking towards the door at the other mums filing in for their special cream tea and wondering when his mum would be coming. It was, without exaggeration, one of the worst guilt pangs I have ever experienced. I attempted to talk myself down from my inner turmoil, reasoning that I had a lot on my plate with a new baby. Besides, perhaps I was overthinking it. Loads of parents are unable to make these things and, with all his friends and all the nursery toys around, he probably wouldn't even have been aware. As he tugged on my jumper to tell me something, I swallowed the lump in my throat and flashed him my best smile.

'We made special Mummy stones for the mummies!'

'Special Mummy *scones*? Did you, darling? That's wonderful.'

'You didn't come.'

*Oh, Jude.*

As we left, hand in hand, with Wilf snoozing in his pram and Henry at our side, banging on about Ender Dragons, I told Jude I was sorry. 'I'll come to the next special tea, poppet. Maybe we could make some scones together at home?' We never did, of course. In fact, I haven't been able to look at a scone the same way since.

I know that I won't be able to go to every Mother's Day treat. I know that sometimes I will be busy working, and that there will be many things I'll miss in the future for all the boys, and that's just life. I also know they probably won't end up emotionally unhinged as adults if I have an important meeting on the day of their class ukulele performance. But I had told Jude that I would be there. He was expecting me and I let him down. Even worse than that, I wasn't even at an important meeting. I was sitting on the sofa eating custard creams and browsing 'People I May Know' on Facebook, while half a mile up the road my little Judy Pops was excitedly waiting for his mummy to turn up and taste the scones he'd made to say thank you for being such a good mummy. I swear to God, the image of Jude's face when he must have realised I wasn't coming will haunt me for ever.

There were many parental-guilt feelings before that Friday, there have been many since and there will be many more still to come. Yet amidst the everyday pangs – I should play with the boys more, I'm not doing enough reading practice with Henry, I should moan about them less, what if the blackcurrant squash I let them have will leave them toothless? – nothing has quite matched the intensity of the Sconegate guilt. I hope it never does!

# Hangovers

An 'adult headache' is a fucker at the best of times. Even in the glory days of youth, when you could just embrace the fact that a hangover meant your entire day would be a write-off, you still had to make it through to bedtime with a banging head, a feeling of nausea and a mouth that tasted (and smelled) like a tiny skunk had found its way in there to die. Then there was the Beer Fear to contend with, as you tried but failed to recall how the evening had ended, your memory drawing a blank directly after you fell off a table in Wetherspoons while attempting to re-enact *Coyote Ugly*.

What I could never have known back then, in the age of Hangover Sundays, was just how much of a luxury those 'write-off' days were. Painful, yes, and often a total waste of a day, too, but the *freedom* to waste a day is one you never appreciate until you find yourself with all the aforementioned hangover symptoms PLUS the added torture of your children, who will jump on you to wake you, poke you in the face then loudly ask what the stamp on your hand is (oh yes, you did, you went *clubbing*, now prepare to regret it).

Children have zero sympathy for Mummy or Daddy's headaches. They won't pop their head in quietly, find you a bit worse for wear then slowly close the door behind them and leave you to have a nap. They won't offer to go out and get you some bacon, full-fat Coke and salt-and-vinegar crisps. Just like the times when you are feeling ill, when you have a hangover, the show must go on. Sometimes you will have to leave the house and, on any occasion when you have failed to check what's on the agenda the following day, you might even find yourself attending a child's birthday party or, worse, going swimming. Getting yourself and your children in and out of swimming costumes in a hot changing-room cubicle is a challenge under normal circumstances – and with a hangover, it's hell.

I've probably had no more than ten proper hangovers in the seven years I've been a parent – and only one biggie since I've been a mother of three. This is partly because I rarely go out nowadays and, if I do, it's likely to be an 'early bird 2 for 1 cocktails' affair where I'm back at home having tea and toast by 9.30 p.m. It's also because, as I've pushed out of my twenties and into my thirties, the post-drinking shame and anxiety has heightened and I've realised that getting drunk to the point of oblivion is completely unnecessary. That said, I also know how easy it is to get carried away, to forget yourself for a moment when you're in the company of friends old or new and you remember, with a warm, fuzzy glow, that feeling of reckless abandonment when shots seem like a good idea.

Just know now, if you have a night out coming up, or if you're craving the big nights out of yesteryear, there are certain things you can do in advance to mitigate the hangover madness/sadness as a parent, even when you have every intention of 'taking it steady'.

- *Stockpile the hangover essentials (Alka-Seltzer, pain relief, carbs), alongside distractions for the kids: magazines with free junk stuck to the cover, sweets, stickers – basically anything that will spoil them into subservience. Buying it all in advance will pay dividends.*

- *On the day of your night out, make sure the kids get plenty of fresh air and exercise. If you bank a long walk through the forest and tire their legs out, you will feel less guilty when you are physically unable to leave the sofa the next day.*

- *Charge the iPad. And your phone. And the Nintendo Switch. And the PlayStation controllers. In fact, charge every device in the house (excluding the adult ones). The fallout from '5 per cent battery remaining' is not something you can be expected to cope with when you're struggling.*

- *By the same token, you should probably take the batteries out of any toys which, on a standard day, make you want to smack your head against a door.*

- *If the shit hits the fan and you wake up feeling a lot like shit that has hit a fan, you'll need to choose your activities wisely. Where possible, instigate games where you get to lie down. Doctors is a good one, though you'll have to insist from the outset that you play the role of 'patient in a coma'. Spies is another hangover favourite because spies have to be very quiet and avoid any sudden movements. If you're really struggling, you might have to crack out the extended version of hide-and-seek, which is extended by them hiding and you never seeking.*

- *Never dwell on the length of the headachy day stretching out in front of you (so many hours, so much pain), or think back to those zero-responsibility hangovers. Instead, mentally break the day down into manageable half-hour chunks.*

- *And remember: shots are never a good idea. Literally, never.*

# Having Another

'About time you had another!'

'When are you planning on giving him a little brother or sister? Be nice for him to have a playmate.'

'Oh, a three-bedroom house, eh? What are you going to do with the *spare* room then?'

'Dry January?' [With a wink] 'Say no more, *mum's* the word.'

These are, apparently, all perfectly reasonable questions for people to ask you as soon as you've had one baby because, now that you're in the club, your future reproductive plans are everybody's business. You are fair game and must expect to engage responsively with anyone who starts talking to you, uninvited, about the perfect age gap between siblings, why you 'mustn't leave it too long' and how selfish it would be of you to have an only child, who will grow up sad, lonely, spoilt and turn into an alcoholic, seeking the company he never got from siblings at the bottom of a bottle.

The 'having another' discussion has always really bugged me. It's different, of course, if you know the person you are chatting with well and would be likely to share with them your long-term family goals anyway.

When it comes to everyone else, it really is none of their business. It's also pretty insensitive of them to ask, even in jest, about when you're planning on providing a sibling for your child when they have no idea whatsoever what's happening behind the scenes. I can only imagine how gut-wrenching 'About time you had another!' is as a conversation starter for someone who has experienced miscarriage or is going through fertility treatment and, more than that, it's ignorant to assume that everybody is going to *want* more than one child. Maybe they're perfectly happy with their lot.

I always wish I'd replied, 'Maybe it's about time you minded your own business?' in response to the having-another interrogation, but I never did. I hope you guys are braver than me.

# Health Visitor

A couple of weeks after the birth, your midwife will usually hand over the care of you and your new baby to a health visitor. For completely irrational reasons, you will treat your health visitor's duty call much the same as you would treat an interview. Certain you are on trial, you will do all manner of unnecessary things ahead of their visit.

Firstly, you will get dressed. Ignoring the fact that you're still bleeding and haven't had more than four hours' sleep in a fortnight, you will put non-pyjama-based clothes on and do something with your hair, convinced that not making an effort will signal to the health visitor that you're not coping.

Once dressed, Operation Tidy-up will commence. You'll hoover and disinfect everything, deeming sparkling surfaces necessary to prove to the health visitor that you take the eradication of germs in the family home extremely seriously.

Someone will be sent out for fresh milk and posh biscuits, which the health visitor will politely decline because the three mums she has seen before you did exactly the same and, besides, she doesn't actually have that much time – she's really just here to have a look at the baby and check you're both getting on OK. She doesn't even look under the sofas or check the kitchen surfaces for germs and you're a bit disappointed she hasn't seemed to notice you've put earrings in for the occasion.

It turns out you're not on trial and she's there to help you, which is wonderful but does mean you wasted an hour getting the place inspection-ready. The only bonus being that there are now posh biscuits in the cupboard. Plus, you might as well take some selfies with the baby, as it would be a shame to let the mascara you've put on go to waste.

# Hypnobirthing

Significantly less wanky than it sounds – in fact, extremely low-ranking on the wanky scale – hypnobirthing is a terrible name for something brilliant. When I wrote my first book, I vowed that, in the unlikely event we were mad enough to have a third child ('as hypothetical as what I'd do if we won the lottery'), I would give hypnobirthing a bash. Well, we were mad enough to have a third child and I did give hypnobirthing a bash, which turned out to be one of the best – if not *the* best – grown-up decision I've ever made (a first-place tie with getting a dishwasher).

I'm not going to write Wilf's birth story here because it would be too long and probably a bit self-indulgent, serving mainly to allow me to bask in the memory of the day, but if you are familiar with my first two birth stories, Jude's in particular, you will know that I have previously been someone who would scream at midwives, swear, demand hard drugs and refuse point-blank to push. So the very fact that I am able to sit here basking in fond birth memories shows you just how much hypnobirthing changed the game for me.

It's not at all the mumbo-jumbo, incense-burning, compulsory placenta-consuming affair I mistakenly thought it would be and, what's more, nobody gets hypnotised. Paul McKenna doesn't even feature. It's actually hugely practical, and the breathing alone was something I will always be thankful I practised. Much better than the hard drugs in the end. Who knew?

You won't get a great deal of genuine advice from me in this book but, if you are pregnant for the first, second, third or tenth time, I cannot recommend hypnobirthing enough.

# Identity

I used to find it a bit nauseating when I heard people say, 'I just don't know who I am any more.' Then I became a mum and, for the first time in my life, I just didn't know who I was any more. Genuinely, I felt like I'd lost myself.

If I'd attempted to retrace my steps to find out when and where I'd misplaced whoever I was before, I reckon there's a strong likelihood I might have found 'the old me' somewhere between the office on my last day of work and the sofa a few months later, sitting with a baby attached to one boob and jammie-dodger crumbs on the other, engrossed in *Rip Off Britain*.

# I

I'm not sure if it's any one thing or a series of things that contribute to that sense of losing one's identity, but I do know from speaking to hundreds of other mums that it's a strange and frightening feeling. It's also very common. You become so consumed by motherhood in all its messy, maddening glory that you can't find the energy for anything else. I remember being adamant that I wasn't going to let motherhood change me – I was having a baby, not a lobotomy! – then, slowly but surely, the bits of me that had become so integral to who I was before having children started to wither a little.

Even without having a baby, being out of work for any number of months would probably have left me feeling a bit lost. I'd learned to value my self-worth in a work context and then, suddenly, there was someone else sitting in my seat, quite literally, making all the decisions I'd previously quite enjoyed making – while I was at home debating the big parenting questions like whether baby-led weaning really was 'saving us time'. (A friend had told me this was one of the 'pros', as then he could just eat whatever I ate, but in reality, my diet wasn't predominately unseasoned, steamed vegetables and, though I hadn't sought an expert opinion, it didn't feel right to be sharing a packet of Frazzles with him).

The relationships I had with pretty much everyone else had changed, too, and it's surprising how much of your identity comes from who you perceive yourself to be to other people. I'd gone from being a good friend, a loving wife, a reliable colleague and an absolute liability on a night out to being someone who just couldn't seem to find the time for anything other than mum-ing. Friends would call and I'd text asking them to call back as I didn't want to risk waking the baby, who'd finally fallen asleep on my chest. James would only have to roll over towards me in bed for a spoon and I'd thrust my pelvis forward and away from him because I didn't want something poking me in the back and reminding me of what we weren't doing any more. (I'm not blaming James for having a spoon-induced stiffy, obviously, that's just nature.)

People had stopped asking for my opinion or insight into anything, and I was glad, to be honest, as I wasn't sure if I had opinions any more. At the doctor's, during mine and Henry's six-week check, the doctor asked about Henry before peering at me over his glasses and asking, 'And how's *Mum* doing?' I'd lost my name, and this was me now. Mum.

As time's ticked on, though, I've realised that I didn't lose who I was – not really – I just went AWOL for a while and returned with a shifted set of priorities and a few new personality traits to match. I'm still a good friend, or at least I hope I am. I'm a bit of a crap lover compared to what I was pre-kids, but the pair of us do give each other something very special occasionally ... the gift of a nap. When I went back to work, I relished being in an environment where people spoke with urgency about things that didn't involve rashes.

And now? Well, for a few years, I've been making a living out of writing about being a mum, so motherhood is not only the chief ingredient of my home identity, it's also been the basis of my employment. It's probable that I've shot myself right in the fanny there and forfeited any right I once had to moan about missing the parts of me that weren't mum-defined ...

# Ikea

Of all the stupid, most twattish things we have ever done as parents, taking three children to Exeter's Ikea the weekend it opened may just be the twattiest of them all.

Hands held up, I only have myself to blame. I was so blind-sided by the thought of browsing Kallax shelving and Ribba frames that I forgot the practicalities of having three small children in tow. It was everything you would imagine Ikea-with-children on a heaving opening weekend to be.

It had started well. Upon entering the store, Henry and Jude were given paper Viking hats and Wilf gurgled merrily at the super-smiley new staff members who were greeting the hordes of weekend flat-packers as they filed in. It was going to be so much fun!

I realised there would be no Kallax browsing the moment I found myself standing in the rug section holding a crying Wilf while James looked for a 'hiding' Jude and Henry declared he was desperate for a poo. Every time we stopped to look at something there was a whinge, a fight or a fart. Jude wanted Henry's Viking hat, despite it being identical to his own. 'Ikea is boring,' they announced. They hated Ikea. Henry was 'starving'. No, Jude didn't want to try the meatballs 'all children love' because he 'only likes nursery meatballs'. Good to know.

They ran around in circles in the display bedrooms, careering into innocent folk who were trying to jot down the item location numbers of bedside tables using one of those Borrower pencils. Jude said 'butt hole'. There were tuts. Wilf filled his nappy. James stopped talking and began communicating non-verbally, clenching his jaw and dragging our still-whingeing children through to the Market Hall, where I didn't get a chance to look at any fake succulents because the let's-throw-the-towel-in line had been crossed and we all just wanted it to end (though I did panic-buy some Tupperware on the way out because I couldn't bear the thought of leaving with nothing). Never again, we vowed, on the way out. 'Not fucking worth it.'

It wasn't until later that I discovered they have a crèche.

# Imposter Syndrome

Perhaps most commonly associated with the workplace, Imposter Syndrome describes a feeling of self-doubt, anxiety and the fear of being discovered as a fraud in whatever professional accomplishments you have achieved or are currently achieving. Despite evidence to the contrary, Imposter Syndrome will have you believe that you don't deserve to be where you are. I have experienced this many times in a work context (and still do, to a certain extent – *I'm not a proper author, any moment now I'm going to get outed*, etc. etc.), but never have I felt more of an imposter than the first time I went to a baby group.

I was convinced that it looked as though I'd been handed a baby at the door and that all the other mums, the proper ones, would smell my fear and incompetence. I didn't fit in. I knew it, they knew it, we all knew it.

It felt surreal to be there. Just a month before, Tuesday mornings would have seen me walking into a sales meeting, notepad and cuppa in hand, calm and in control of my life. Now here I was, stumbling through the door of the 'Stay and Play' group, dishevelled, sweaty and in control of precisely nothing, with a new boss who was 1.7 feet tall and extremely angry with me for not putting my tits in his mouth quickly enough. This had never once happened in my previous job.

At its peak, this mum-based Imposter Syndrome made me feel like I couldn't (and perhaps shouldn't) join in with conversations with other mums because they would catch me out. I wasn't good enough, I didn't know enough and I hadn't earned my right to be there. In hindsight, this was a ridiculous notion – nobody had more right to be there than anybody else – but you obviously can't help how you feel, and I felt like a fraud.

I'm not sure that feeling of fraudulence ever fully leaves you, but I've come to realise it's perhaps less about not feeling good enough or worthy enough as a *mother* and more about not feeling good enough or worthy enough as an *adult*. It still seems strange to me, seven years in, that I am (jointly) responsible for the care, safety and wellbeing of three human beings. School parents' evening is a classic – we sit on tiny chairs to talk to a teacher and it seems nothing short of ludicrous that *we* are the parents when it was only five minutes ago* that we were last at primary school ourselves. There must be some mistake.

If Parental Imposter Syndrome rings true to you, then you should know this. There is no mistake. Nobody is going to catch you out. You are the parent. It's fucking brilliant and terrifying all at once.

# Instamums

Trendy wall to pose in front of – check. Peace sign – check. Children in extortionate (but ethically sound) clothing – check. Motivational message about being a 'mum boss' – check. Bonus points can be achieved by posting pictures of antique floor tiles, peonies, babies wearing bloomers and/or bonnets as though they're extras from a period drama, retreats with a 'girl gang' in the country, an OOTD (that's 'outfit of the day', to you and me), some kind of a campaign message with its own T-shirt and flat-lays of fancy breakfasts,

. . . . . . . . . . . .

\* It's been more than twenty years since I left primary school. How the hell did that happen?

ideally featuring smashed avocado and an oozing poached egg #motherhoodrising #mumsthatslay #capturingmotherhood #thehashtagsneverrelatetothepicture #orindeedanything #nooneknowswhattheymean

It's all right, I'm allowed to take the piss out of the above formula because the papers say I, too, am an 'Instamum' – I just let the side down by being more likely to share pictures of kids' artwork that looks like penises rather than peonies. I must try harder.

# Jeggings

A cross between jeans and leggings, these are a staple of the postpartum wardrobe. They'll give the illusion that you've put proper clothes on and therefore have your shit together and yet you can just pull them on, like leggings. It's a revelation. None of that jumping up and down to do the zip up on your skinniest pair of jeans malarkey. In a world full of new enemies – underwire, light-coloured denim (see Leakage) and lace – jeggings are your new best friend.

# Juggling

For a long while, 'It's a bit of a juggle, isn't it?' was my textbook response to anyone who asked me how I was finding motherhood. Though not untrue, 'a bit of a juggle' is a massive fucking understatement. Parenting is a lot of a juggle. The juggliest of juggles. Like trying to juggle slippery fish while walking across a tightrope in heels. Backwards.

The biggest problem with this particular juggle is that as soon as you think you've got it all under control, when the balls are finally all in the air and you're probably not sleeping but, hey, at least you're not dropping any, something happens to rock the boat. Somebody gets poorly, everybody gets poorly, the car gives up, your shifts change at work, the baby starts teething – these can all knock your routine off track. However, by far the worst organisation demolisher when it comes to an otherwise manageable juggle is the school holidays.

A time to be cherished, of course. A time to spend going on trips and making dens and getting to know each other a little better outside of the confines of the school week. The problem comes when you've just about got your act together based on a schedule for a 'normal week' and then – wallop – the school holidays roll around and take a massive dump all over your schedule. If you work, this presents a logistical nightmare regarding childcare and, if you don't work, it presents an emotional nightmare as, suddenly, the system you've carved out to keep the family ship sailing smoothly flies out the window, along with all the food in the cupboards, which will disappear in seconds because children expect snacks between meals and sometimes snacks between snacks.

School holidays can sometimes also bring with them the realisation that your children don't like each other very much. You then have to add 'mediating fights' to your daily juggle list and it's not always an easy one to keep on top of. Take your eye off the ball for a second to watch *This Morning* and there'll be a tussle that goes too far, resulting in a chokeslam that nearly kills someone.

The only practical way to get through the school holidays with any sliver of sanity intact is to accept that you'll need to let some of the usual in-air balls drop and resume your normal juggle when term begins again. Or clone yourself, where I imagine you'd need at least two and a half of you just to keep things ticking over.

# Jumperoo

Aka the Circle of Neglect, the Chair of Neglect, the Poo-peroo and 'that giant plastic monstrosity in our living room' (my husband, 2018).

If you've never seen one, a Jumperoo is something you sit babies in where they can bounce themselves up and down, surrounded by garishly bright activity attachments while listening to 'fun' jungle / rainforest sounds.

On a good day, this contraption will afford you up to fifteen minutes' peace to have a hot cup of tea, tidy the kitchen or go to the toilet. You can do those things safe in the knowledge that the baby can't get out, or choke.

On a bad day, your baby will liberate the three days' build-up of poo they've been saving and, because you've had your face in a coffee or have been bleaching the sink, you'll only notice when it's too late and they're already doing baby Riverdance in a puddle of excrement. Due to the bouncing motion, which assists in the rapid and wide-reaching spread of devastation, a Jumperoo poo is just about the worst poo-tastrophe you can encounter. You won't know where to start with the clean-up operation and your gut instinct will be to conclude that you're just going to have to throw the whole lot out, including the baby.

# Junk Modelling

In child-development terms, junk modelling, which is effectively the creation of kids' artwork out of stuff you'd usually bung in the recycling, is a hugely positive activity. It offers young children the chance to explore their creativity using a range of props and materials to create a masterpiece straight from their mind's eye. Fantastic!

What it means for the parent, though, is that their child returns from nursery, pre-school or the childminder with cereal boxes taped to toilet-roll tubes covered in milk-carton lids. You won't have a clue what it's supposed to 'be' – it looks like your bin threw up and then someone painted it – but you must be encouraging of their new-found skills, so you will ask them to tell you all about it. With any luck, you'll have a kid with a fantastic imagination who'll tell you it's a telescope or an old radio set or part of a spaceship. Alternatively, you'll have a child like my Henry who will say, 'It's just a Coco Pops box with loo rolls and lids stuck on it.' Right-o.

What you then do with these creations is something of a dilemma. The first couple of times the boys' artwork came home, I told myself that I would keep it all. You'd have to be cold-hearted and cruel to throw it away – look at the effort that went into sticking ten pipe cleaners in one clump in the middle of the box! The trouble is, over time, these masterpieces start piling up and, if you have two or more children, you start to realise you're in grave danger of drowning in a sea of poster-painted abstract art.

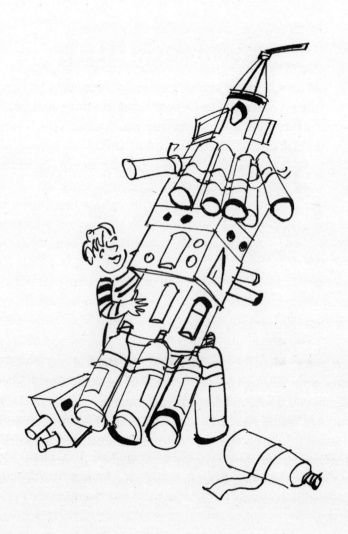

# J

Thankfully, there are a few things you can do to lessen both the volume of artwork and the associated guilt of 'recycling' some of it:

- *Firstly, work out a system. How are you going to prioritise which pieces to keep? For us, 'firsts' are always kept (even the single crayon squiggle on an A4 sheet with a bit of yoghurt on it), as are Mother's Day/ Father's Day cards, as these are small and easy to store in a box under the bed with the family photos you'll never get around to sorting into albums.*

- *Special pieces, or those drawings that actually look quite good (i.e. not those from the era when Henry would only draw 'mazes' in thick black felt tip) can be framed.*

- *A line of string with mini pegs is a great way to hang up the most recent pictures and these can be refreshed when new bits come in.*

- *Everything else is fair game for the chop.*

If you feel bad for chucking stuff out, think ahead to twenty years' time. Though possible, it's highly unlikely your child will ever sit you down and demand to know the location of the 756 works of art he presented you with over a fifteen-year period. A small folder of the best or most sentimental artwork is plenty. Plus, the 'junk' is rarely washed properly before modelling so not throwing it out presents a health risk. You're doing the best by everyone.

# Kids' Parties

Ten facts about kids' parties:

1. *Nobody wants to be there. Least of all the parents of the child whose birthday it is.*

2. *Alongside friends who are known to you, your child will occasionally get invited to the birthday parties of children they have never mentioned. Sometimes this is a 'making up numbers' exercise when Birthday Child's mum and dad have hired a hall and some inflatables and don't want it to look empty. You are, of course,*

extremely grateful to be going to a kids' party at 3 p.m. on a Sunday, but feel slightly aggrieved that you have to spend the morning shopping around for a present to give to a child you've never heard of. You will end up in TK Maxx, where you will buy something obscure that you're certain they won't like but that looks pretty decent for £5.

3. Birthday-party buffets are a unique shade of beige. A bit like the chicken nuggets, chips and potato smilies you serve up at home, but somehow less well cooked and more anaemic. Even the pizza is beige.

4. As an adult, you're not supposed to help yourself to the buffet until all the kids have lost interest and it is clear there is some going spare. Sorting yourself out with your own plate at the outset is frowned upon.

5. If the parents hosting have made a pass-the-parcel, you'd better pray to God that they've put a mini pack of Haribo between every layer and done enough layers for every child in the circle. If they haven't, or if Uncle Geoff, who's in charge of party music fails to stop on a different child each time and little Bobby ends up with two packets of sweets when Lola hasn't had any, there will be a scene.

6. If there are party games, it's easy to become emotionally involved. You can try your best to act nonchalant but will secretly be raging when Shannon wins Musical Statues, beating your child, who was clearly the most unmoving out of the last two. It's a fix.

7. While most of the modern party music and accompanying dance crazes will confuse you, you'll be

K

pleasantly surprised to find that 'Superman', the classic party song you remember from your own seventh birthday party, is still going strong. You may find you remember all the actions. If it's one of those decent kids' parties where there's wine, you'll probably end up skiing, spraying [the deodorant] and Macho Man-ing. You have to take your fun where you can get it nowadays.

8. You will be impressed and horrified, in equal measure, at the dance aptitude of young girls who stand in rows doing the moves to 'Watch Me (Whip/Nae Nae)'. (If you don't yet know it, you will when you get on the kids' party scene.) Later, after watching a ten-year-old in hot-pants twerk, you'll conclude that kids, particularly girls, are growing up far too quickly. You will be glad to see them back in uniform on Monday when they've wiped that muck off their faces.

9. Regardless of whether or not there is a dance floor, boys will skid on their knees. This has been happening for decades, centuries probably, which is just as well because everyone knows knee-sliding is a sure-fire way of looking super-cool.

10. Party bags will contain the following: bubbles, stickers, a balloon, a small bouncy ball that presents a choking hazard and a sliver of birthday cake wrapped in a napkin. Whichever sibling wasn't invited to the birthday party will become fixated on the contents of the party bag, purely because it's not theirs. The 'balloon from Riley's party' will pop three days later and everyone will cry.

# Kissing

I smother all three of my boys with kisses, all the time. I can't pick Wilf up for a hip-carry without kissing the top of his little head and, though I sometimes have to catch Henry and Jude first these days, they don't escape kisses from their old mum either.

Of course, I never kiss them on *the lips* because that's disgusting. Imagine kissing your own child on his or her lips? Inappropriate. I am of course referring to the ridiculous online uproar caused when the Beckhams posted pictures of them kissing their kids on the lips. Apparently, it was very 'divisive'. The divide being between those who felt it was perfectly acceptable to kiss your own children on the lips (i.e. normal people) and those whose brains are worryingly wired to sexualise the relationship between parent and child, then take to the internet to blame the parent. What a time to be alive.

# Knobhead

Something you must never call your child, apparently.

# Leakage

There is so much that can leak after you have kids and, other than an upside-down Tommee Tippee beaker that doesn't have its lid on properly, this leakage is mostly bodily fluid related.

First you leak blood and whatever leftovers are in your uterus. Granted, this can be managed with maternity pads or Tena lady pants, but at some stage there will be seepage from the leakage and you'll find yourself throwing Vanish at the crotch of your fave pair of pyjama bottoms. That has never once been something I've seen another mum do in an advert.

Then there's the breast-milk leakage, which predominately occurs when your milk comes in and your boobs go crazy, or when you find yourself away from your baby at a time you would normally feed them (including when they're sleeping and your boobs are screaming that it's time for the next feed). Again, this can be managed, with breast pads (there are some cracking washable ones available nowadays, too) and, after a while, things settle down, but it's a breastfeeding rite of passage to wake up with a soaked bra and T-shirt which, when dried, will smell a bit like a lunchbox left in a school bag for a week.

Perhaps the worst and longest-lasting leakage is that of the bladder variety. You should listen when people tell you to do your pelvic-floor exercises (and, obviously, seek help if you are having incontinence problems). One thing I have learned is that even if you *think* you are fine in that department and have had no significant mishaps for a while, if you push your luck and try to 'hold it', you will wet yourself in M&S Simply Food. True story, I'm afraid.

# Listening

I love my children with all my heart, however, I think I would *like* them a whole lot more if they just listened every once in a while. How hard can it be to listen? Genuine question, because I find my kids' inability/unwillingness to listen to anything that comes out of my mouth absolutely baffling. Nine times out of ten, whenever I find myself shouting at them, I am shouting because nobody fucking listened the first eleven times I didn't shout.

I always start with a reasonable request in my reasonable voice, which has a reasonable tone. I'll often inject a chuckle, just to show them that I'm still fun, I just have to do the boring parent thing, too.

'Guys, can you keep the noise down a tiny bit? It's early and I don't think next door need to hear your wrestling finishing moves before they've had breakfast!'

The reasonable tone continues for a few more minutes, until an edge of exasperation starts to creep in. 'Are you listening, guys? I said, keep the noise down. Why are you shouting?!'

Next comes desperation, where I change tack to a softer plea. Occasionally, there will be begging. 'Please, boys. I don't want to lose my temper but you're *this* close to Mummy getting very cross. I am asking you nicely: please just calm down a bit.'

Finally, following a screech or a cry or something that tips me over the edge, I'll flip and shout, 'FOR GOD'S SAKE, WILL YOU PACK IT IN! Why is nobody listening to me? Jesus Christ! I'm banning wrestling and telly and food for a week! And you can forget about Christmas, because it's cancelled!'

Cue lots of crying, from everyone, and an entire scene which could have been avoided. If. They. Had. Just. Bloody. Listened.

One has to wonder whether it's more the case that they *can* listen, they just selectively tune out the voices they hear most often. In our house, that's both my voice and their dad's voice, as we do a pretty even split of parenting. This means they don't really seem to hear what either of us are saying a lot of the time, frequently resulting in us both shouting, which gets very chaotic.

The top five ignored requests for us are as follows:

1. *'Can you turn it down a bit, please?!'*

   *Said when they are watching* Nicky, Ricky, Dicky and Dawn *at a volume that is making the whole house shake. Of course, it is possible they genuinely might not hear this instruction, due to the racket of the telly, but it's convenient that they always seem to snap back into hearing mode the second I incorrectly call it 'Mickey, Tricky, Dicky and Dom' just to annoy them.*

2. *'Henry, have you got your book bag?'*

   *He never has his book bag, despite several 'Don't forget your book bag' warnings every single school day.*

3. *'Has anyone seen … ?'*

   *[Insert misplaced object that was last seen being moved from its rightful place by one of them.] They will completely ignore requests to assist in the search for said lost object unless it's the TV remote, in which case they'll 'help' by throwing the sofa cushions on the floor.*

4. *'That's enough of that [game] now, it's getting too physical and someone is going to get hurt.'*

   *Spoiler alert: someone gets hurt.*

5. *'Put your shoes on!'*

   *Repeat until you feel like lobbing the shoes at their heads.*

# Lucky

In the six years I have been dicking around on the internet, I have complained about my children a lot. Too much, probably, though in the heat of the sleep-refusing, whingeathon moments, any such complaining on my part has always come from a genuine place of exasperation. Sometimes I have posted when I've been at the very end of my tether, and I mean the *very* end #cantputupwiththisshit. There was the week the whole house was poorly and, by some unfortunate coincidence, mine and James's flu coincided with the boys' gastroenteritis, so, instead of hibernating in bed, I found myself on my hands and knees cleaning up the aftermath of a child's projectile diarrhoea from the skirting boards. Weeks 4–8 of baby Wilf's life (yep, pretty much a whole month), when I just couldn't work out how to make him happy and filmed a series of desperate Instagram stories where I cried over the top of his crying. The time baby Jude fed once every hour through the night and I was so tired I started hallucinating that our blinds were falling down. The time toddler Henry lay down on the floor of the forest, halfway around a one-mile 'fun walk', and refused to move, resulting in me dragging him all the way back to the car park by his hood because I was eight months pregnant with Jude and already feeling twinges.

I often post my gripes without thinking – in many ways, that's why the blog worked, because it was an uncensored account of my parenting life in real time, as events unfolded. The problem with not filtering what you say, or not sitting on your hands for a while to stop you posting in a fit of fury, is that people then think you moan all the time. I know this is what people think of me because they have told me so, in messages, comments, emails and one time to my face at a literary festival, but that's a story for another day. The comments around the moany content of what I post tends to be along the following lines:

*Are you ever happy when you're with your kids?*
*You're always complaining about them!*
*Why did you have kids if they're such a burden?*
*Can't believe you're having another baby when you don't even like the kids you've already got …*

113

I can take the above kind of comments on the chin. They usually prompt an eye roll and an under-the-breath 'piss off' but, ultimately, I'm not bothered – they're less hurtful than the time someone said being pregnant made me look like Slimer from *Ghostbusters*.

However, there is one particular comment that I've written about before and which crops up time and again on some kind of cycle (so if I haven't had one for a while, I know it's only a matter of time). It's one I find a lot harder to ignore: *You don't know how lucky you are.*

Boom. If the intention is to make me feel bad, to make me doubt what I am sharing (and why I am sharing it), then this one-liner hits the bullseye every time. It takes all my self-control to not reply defensively to every such comment. To correct their assumption. To make them understand. I *need* them to understand.

I do know how lucky I am. I really do. I have three lovely boys who I love beyond measure. I thank my lucky stars (and James's sperm) that they are mine for keeps. I would swim through shark-infested mushroom soup (a mash-up of my two phobias right there) to save them. When I die, whatever else I have achieved, they will remain the part of my life I am most proud of. I honestly couldn't be any more grateful.

However, not every day is a #blessed kind of day and the you-don't-know-how-lucky-you-are brigade have got it wrong to believe that vocalising the #notsoblessed days makes you ungrateful on a wider level.

Sometimes kids are tossers. Truly, they are.

Sometimes, something happens to momentarily make me question why we didn't just get a dog.

Sometimes, no matter how hard I'm trying to 'cherish every moment', the moments turn out to be a bit fucking uncherishy.

So yes, I do know how lucky I am but, sometimes, it's testing, and I have a habit of telling everyone just how testing I've found it.

That's OK, I think.

Hope so, anyway.

# Me Time

I was in the queue waiting to pay for a Meal Deal in Boots recently when I overheard a mum telling a friend on the phone that she was heading off on a spa weekend with some girl-friends. It was long overdue 'me time' she said, as she'd not had a moment to herself for two weeks and, the last time, she'd only escaped for a couple of hours to have a mani-pedi. She was frazzled. She needed a couple of days to 'reset' herself away from her kids, who would benefit from her coming back as 'the very best version of herself'. I wondered what a better version of herself would look like.

# M

If I'd been a first-time mum, I'm certain I would have taken an immediate dislike to Mrs Me Time. I would have struggled not to sneer at her mentions of mani-pedis and weekends with the girls. In fact, I can remember texting my husband when I was on my second maternity leave to say, 'There's a woman at Stay and Play who still has her hair coloured every six weeks. My hair is a nest. A NEST.' I don't think he replied, or perhaps the message got lost between the one telling him baby Jude had been sick in my ear and the one that was simply ten rows of crying emojis.

However, as I stood behind her waiting for a self-service checkout to become free, I realised I admired her. I wanted to shout 'Yes!' and high-five her for the unapologetic delivery of the news that she needed some time away from her kids. I've lost count of the number of times I have felt the need to add some kind of defensive side note when announcing any plans not involving the kids. 'Yes, we are asking the grandparents to babysit for the evening, but it's only because we never managed to do anything for our anniversary – it's really an annual thing! We hardly ever leave them.' I don't know for sure why I do this but I think it stems from feeling guilty about wanting to spend time away from them, and if more people spoke like this woman did perhaps we'd stop the extra justification and just say, 'Yep we're having a night off. Can't wait!'

A spa weekend with the girls is not an achievable level of me time for everyone, of course, but even if our me-time expectations vary, the end goal is the same: to feel more refreshed after a break from your parental responsibilities. I had no doubt that when she returned following a weekend of exfoliation and steaming she would indeed be more adept at firefighting the tears and tantrums her kids delivered, just as I feel better equipped to firefight tantrums after an unaccompanied trip to the supermarket. Seriously, a quick browse of the homeware without having to shout, 'Don't touch anything!' restores my Zen nowadays. The last time I had a smear test I was grateful for the lie-down.

We really ought not to apologise for wanting some time out. It's not a bad idea to try and 'reset' ourselves every once in a while. I often feel like I need a master reset, a massive rebooting that will restore my brain to factory settings and let me start again. A spa weekend with the girls would probably do that but, in the meantime, a quick glide around Asda on my own is enough to close a few brain browsers. Take what you can get.

# Mental Health

I have always been a pretty open book when it comes to the things I have found difficult about being a mum. I struggled with a lot of what parenting threw at me the first time around and, although to a lesser extent, I struggled the second time, too. Those struggles formed the very basis of what I wrote about on the blog.

Like many mums, I was unsure about what I was supposed to be doing. I felt exhausted. I missed talking about things that weren't baby-bowel-movement related and I felt guilty for sometimes wishing I could put the baby down without him immediately crying to come back up again. Alongside the many good days, there were days where my sole focus was getting everybody to the end of the day in one piece.

'It sounds like you've got a spot of postnatal depression, is there someone you can talk to?' came a reply from a very kind (and concerned) follower on one of my blog posts. I mulled that thought over for a while, wondering if perhaps she was right. Maybe I'd got it wrong thinking that it was 'normal' to feel the levels of frustration I sometimes felt. Perhaps it *wasn't*

OK to lose my shit or cry or daydream about walking out of the door after a particularly intense teething bout from Jude coincided with Henry's peak 'Don't like it' phase. Yet I had spoken to a huge number of mums who had experienced postnatal depression or postnatal anxiety and I think I knew, deep down, that despite finding motherhood exceptionally testing at times, on a more fundamental level my mental health was faring OK.

When I was pregnant for the third time, therefore, I wasn't at all worried about my mental health. I'd done it twice before and, with the virtual back-up of thousands of mums who'd said 'We find this hard, too!', it felt like the pressure was off a bit. My expectations were more realistic, I felt more relaxed about doing it all again and I knew I wouldn't beat myself up in the way I had done previously if I found myself struggling. Besides, our circumstances had changed pretty radically since having Henry and Jude and, for the first time, it would be James, not me, doing the biggest parental-leave stint. I would only be taking a couple of months off before heading back to work and leaving the men in my life together at home. All the ducks were in a row to make baby three the easiest baby yet.

The thing about mental health, however, is that it doesn't give a shit about your ducks. It cares not that you seem to have everything in place to ensure the family cogs turn effectively (as best you can) when the new baby arrives, nor that previous experience has taught you to put less pressure on yourself to be the 'perfect mum'. I have read so many times, from so many wonderful people who have spoken up about their own experiences, that depression and anxiety *do not discriminate* and yet, despite this, and despite the number of times I have shared such messages, for some foolish reason I still considered myself to be someone who wouldn't have any trouble with my own mental health.

It consequently came as a bit of a shock when I started feeling out of sorts a few months after Wilf was born. The 'baby blues' the health visitor had advised might strike on Day 5 seemed to have bypassed me, picking up momentum and some extra blue force and then returning to whack me in the face somewhere nearer to Day 65. It was very different from any of the postnatal feelings I'd had before and, because there was no 'reason' for me to feel blue (another foolish notion), I tried to rationalise how I felt. I was tired, I'd taken on a bit too much too soon after the birth, it must be the hormones. In truth, though it's likely the general unease I was feeling was exacerbated by trying to do too much too soon on the work front, there was an underlying level of anxiety that had become more of an issue than I wanted to admit. I was hugely fortunate that it wasn't long-lasting, no more than a couple of months, in the end – though a couple of months feels like a couple of years when you are in the thick of something you would rather not be in the thick of! I was also hugely fortunate that I felt able to talk to James, who'd sensed that all might not be well, though, even then, it was hard to explain what I was feeling.

No one thing was 'wrong', as such. It wasn't that I felt unable to get up and face the day, nor that I was having trouble bonding with Wilf. It was more a feeling of anxiety underneath everything I was doing, like a base layer, that I couldn't shake off. The best way I can describe it is to say it was as if a doom cloud had descended. I had a terrible feeling that something bad was going to happen and I couldn't seem to budge the nervy tummy butterflies that I was most used to getting before an interview or when I knew I had to do a presentation at work. I also found that rather than craving escape from the house, as had happened with Henry and Jude, I needed to be closer to home. Twice, I cut short work trips to get on an earlier train back home, and I found myself making excuses not to go to things because they would mean not being at home.

I found there was lots of advice available online and, because the cloud started to lift before too long, and James checked in with me regularly for 'doom cloud status' updates, I didn't get to a stage where I felt I needed anything more in the way of professional help (though, in hindsight, that couldn't have hurt). It was something I chose not to share on social media – in all honesty, I drafted several 'doom cloud' posts, but I think I was terrified such a post would attract attention that would make me feel more anxious or, worse, that people would think *I* was trying to attract attention, which was so far from the truth. However, I am writing this here in case it speaks to someone who right now is feeling a bit out of sorts. It is OK to lose your shit, it is fine to have the odd cry, it is normal to be at your wits' end with the kids, but existing under a doom cloud is not right and, if that's where you are right now, please tell someone.* You are not on your own.

# Mornings

I quite like the school run. Perhaps it's because I don't do it every day, though I usually do three drop-offs out of five each week, and one of those is Monday, so I'm *at least* 60 per cent qualified to have school-run feelings. (I imagine you get extra points for Mondays.)

In the infants, the school run also involved taking Henry into his classroom and staying for five minutes to help him with

. . . . . . . . . . . .

* I'll list a few resources at the end of this book.

early work set by the teacher. Sometimes this was reading together, sometimes it was a little maths puzzle. I genuinely love doing that stuff, as I'm always aware that so many parents miss out on doing school runs through work schedules that don't allow for a 9.15 to 3 working day. My schedule doesn't allow for it either, to be honest, but there's nobody to tell me off or sack me when I roll in flustered at 9.30. I just end up working in the evenings to claim back the time I spent doing phonics, which is a trade I am happy with.

What I don't enjoy, in any way, shape or form, is the hour and a half to two hours of bedlam that occurs before the actual school run. A gigantic amount of shit can go down before the front door is closed and, much like the hour or two before bedtime (see Witching Hour), a concentrated window of bedlam makes everything seem more frantic, as demonstrated by the below snapshot of our morning routine.

### Monday, 14 January 2019

6.52: Jude's shout of 'Finished!' (an invitation to wipe his bum) wakes the whole house. The morning has begun.

7.05: Henry and Jude sit on the sofa in their pyjamas, staring at the telly. Their clothes piles (school clothes for Henry, plain clothes for Jude, as he doesn't have nursery on Mondays), lay untouched on the floor, despite my encouragement that they should get dressed straight away to save time later.

7.11: Realise Wilf has done a poo that has leaked through all his layers. Henry and Jude complain about the stench, while also asking where their toast is. Their toast is burning in the toaster.

7.25: James remakes the toast, with 'honey *and* butter' for Henry and 'jam *and* butter' for Jude. He then gets ready to leave for work, as I resist the urge to hang on to his ankles.

7.31: Attempt to wrestle Wilf into a clean vest that isn't covered in excrement. Discover he has excrement on his foot, which he has kicked on to my tights. Do a quick wet-wipe of the tights and pretend to myself that I will change them before we leave the house.

7.35: Feed Wilf a pouch of fruit and some Cheerios.

7.42: Wipe buttery-jam and buttery-honey off the sofa. Wave goodbye to James.

7.50: Tell the bigger boys that they can play for half an hour before school if they get their clothes on and their teeth brushed.

7.56: Hear hysterical laughter from upstairs, prompting a quick check on how the teeth-brushing is going. Discover Henry creased up on the floor, laughing at Jude, who thought it would be funny to 'brush his face' rather than his teeth, resulting in a toothpaste beard.

8.02: Grab a fruit snack to put in Henry's book bag and find homework we haven't done. Shout upstairs to Henry that we need to do it immediately. This is met with a protest about how unfair his life is and how I promised him he could play for half an hour and now I'm breaking my promise.

8.10: Coerce Henry into doing his homework, which is all about identifying common nouns, while simultaneously picking toothpaste out of Jude's ear and trying to stop Wilf eating Steve from the *Minecraft* Lego set.

8.17: Start shouting at everybody that if we're not careful, we're going to be late. Inform Henry that I think 'there' might be an adverb rather than a common noun. He starts crying at me because they haven't done adverbs yet.

8.23: Get the pram out of the garage, put coats and shoes by the door and collect the hastily finished homework, ignoring the glaring adverb/common noun confusion. Conclude that we just might make it out on time after all.

8.29: Observe Wilf going red and gurning. Confirm, with a sniff, that he has managed to squeeze out another pootastrophe. Repeat the nappy-changing wrestle from 7.31.

8.32: Shout loudly, about everything, while flapping arms in a panic, 'Toilet! Shoes! Coats! Book bag!'

8.38: Realise I can't find the keys. They are nowhere logical. Consider leaving house unlocked but watched something scary on the telly and now have a fear of people breaking in, not to burgle but to hide in the loft or in cupboards until night-time. Decide being late for school is favourable to being butchered in our beds.

8.47: Locate the keys. Drag all three children out of the door. Strap Wilf into pram.

8.48: Notice Jude's shoes are on the wrong feet. Sit him down on front steps to swap shoes. Mutter under breath about being late.

8.53: Get halfway to school before realising I've forgotten to lock the door anyway. Decide to risk the bed-butchering.

# Moving House

Anyone who's ever undertaken a house move will agree that it's a stressful life event. We moved house twice before we had kids and I can remember feeling moderately stressed both times; overwhelmed by all the sale/purchase paperwork and constantly living in fear that some twat in the chain would pull out. It's hard work packing up a house around work shifts and, invariably, your target exchange and completion dates are pushed back at the last minute, so the week you'd booked off work, and which you'd planned to spend settling in to your new pad, becomes a week where you stare angrily at boxes in the old house, sending an email every hour to your estate agent and solicitor stressing your keenness to move.

When we moved for the third time, this time with a one-year-old Henry, I remember it being roughly the same level of stress as the first two times – I certainly don't remember it being much worse, though we had accumulated significantly more crap. Fast-forward then to last year, when we undertook the moving adventure with a six-year-old, a three-year-old and an eight-month-old in tow and, oh em gee, I'm surprised *we* didn't become those twats in the chain who pulled out. It was all kinds of horrendous from start to finish.

Firstly, there were the viewings on our existing property. We'd had a huge tidy-up so the house would look amazing in the photos and stupidly had allowed ourselves to believe that we'd manage to keep everything in order during the viewings period. Toys were put in fancy storage baskets. Shoes were put away. Dinners were no longer eaten on laps and flowers were bought from Tesco to shove in a vase on the table and make the place look dead fancy. This lasted for twenty-four hours before we realised that trying to keep a house tidy with kids in it is unachievable (see Tidying Up). We changed tactic and decided we'd just give the place a quick spruce-up on the day of the viewings. Which was fine until we received a call at 3 p.m. one day to say, 'Mrs Castle would like to pop round and see the house at 4 p.m., is that OK?' to which we said, 'Erm, yes, not a problem,' before running around in circles screaming 'Fuucccck!!!' while trying to make the house look less like the aftermath of a raucous Busy Bees session at playgroup. Something I'd read online said you should put a drop of vanilla essence in the oven and warm it for ten minutes prior to any viewings, so the prospective buyer would get a waft of home baking when they stepped through the door. I *would* have done that, had I not been busy trying to Febreze the whole of downstairs in a desperate attempt to prevent Mrs Castle from getting a waft of *eau de* farty boys when she stepped through the door.

It's not just keeping the house tidy that becomes a problem when you have kids at large, it's also being able to vacate the house at the drop of a hat so people can have a look around. Luckily, our house went on the market in the spring, so we could at least escape and do laps of the park, which was close enough to the old place for us to peer down the road and see if they'd left yet. I know it's all part of the process, it's what you expect, but walking around a park with kids who are whingeing because it's their teatime gets annoying, even more so when you get home to discover that Mr Barriball liked the property overall but wasn't keen on the lack of a fourth bedroom, despite the fact that he'd known there wasn't a fourth fucking bedroom before he viewed it.

Then comes the packing, which is impossible to do when you're in charge of children, firstly, because they don't let you do any task for more than fifteen seconds and, secondly, because if they see you packing anything that belongs to them, even stuff they *never* play with, they unpack it and declare that they can't live with it being in a box for two weeks.

Finally, when you do make it to 'the other side', your children will see you with your hands full of bags and boxes, stressing about how you can't work out the new heating system and *Oh god, where are the keys for the windows?*, and then choose that moment to say, 'Can I have a snack?' You'll realise then that they have no clue whatsoever that a house move is one of the most stressful life events one can go through and that having kids wailing, 'Mum, he's annoying me!' makes it even more stressful. They couldn't give any less of a shit about whether it's been stressful or not, quite frankly, they just want some Pom-Bears.

One thing I *will* say in celebration of having kids with you during the house-moving adventure is that when you're looking around possible houses, once you've got past the obvious test of stopping them from breaking anything, they might just help you to see the potential of a house that you may otherwise have overlooked. The house we moved to last year was (and still is) a massive project. I don't mean it needed a bit of a paint, I mean I posted a picture of it on Instagram and someone messaged to tell me it looked like Wetherspoons crossed with Fred and Rosemary West's house. Yet when Jude trundled in on our first viewing, he ignored the brown-and-yellow patterned carpet teamed with garish floral wallpaper in the hallway, asked us to open the back door (which is a wooden panel you unbolt and slide – yes, really), and went straight outside to play. When we went upstairs, he saw what would be his room to share with his big brother, at the time with bright pink wallpaper and green carpet, and said, 'It's a big bedroom, Mummy!' before looking out of the window and telling me to come quick because he could see 'the cathedral and John Lewis!' in the distance. We knew we'd have a huge job on our hands doing the place up and that the sensible option would be to buy a new-build that was 'done', but I could picture us all there, in the garden during the summer, the boys playing in their bedroom, and I'm sure watching Jude potter around like he already owned the place helped with that.

If you've got a big move coming up, just know you *will* get through it and it will all be worth it. Eventually. Apparently. It just might not seem worth it when you find yourselves without a bathroom for three weeks, sleeping on mattresses in the living room and surviving with one hob ring to cook dinner for five.

All right, I'm 50 per cent regretting not getting the new-build, if I'm honest.

# Mum Type

I was talking at a book event a couple of years ago when the interviewer asked me, with a tilt to the head: 'What *type* of mum are you, do you think?'

I was momentarily stupefied. I know the question hadn't been posed with the intention of catching me off guard. In fact, the interviewer and I had been getting on famously and it was because of this that I stuttered and stumbled my way through a description of the 'sort' of parent I thought I was, keen to answer her question, before stopping myself and replying simply, 'A good one, hopefully.'

On reflection, it was just a question. Perhaps she thought I would answer that I'm a laid-back mum rather than a strict mum, or that I'm a disorganised mum, or maybe that I'm a mum who is turning into my own mum (to be fair, all of those are true enough). Yet for some reason it jarred as a question and, as I sat on a train home tucking into a balanced dinner of Pickled Onion Monster Munch and Percy Pigs, I realised that it was the whole 'type of mum' part that didn't sit well with me.

My issue with it was twofold. On a basic level, I don't much like mums being labelled as any one 'type', as it leads to us making assumptions about them more generally, based entirely on that one flaky label. I know this because I am guilty of having made those assumptions before. I have heard about a friend of a friend who is an 'Earth Mother' or the sister of a colleague who is a 'Pushy Mum' and I immediately feel like I know more about them than I actually do. I've been convinced, mistakenly, that I wouldn't have anything in common with those mums because they are not my *type*. I have come to realise that doing so is narrow-minded and means I risk missing out on friendships with women I have loads in common with, outside of any arbitrary label.

The second reason, and the main reason I struggled so much to answer the question, is that I honestly couldn't tell you what 'type' of mum I am. Not succinctly, anyway. Sure, I probably have a parental personality you could profile somehow, with preferences and tendencies that make it easier to fit me into one box over another. Yet if you plotted it all on one of those spider diagrams, the outcome of that profile could vary drastically depending on what day you catch me on. I am a different mum on different days. I am a different kind of mum depending on what activity I am doing. I am a different kind of mum depending on how I am feeling. I am a different kind of mum depending on whether my kids have slept and, in turn, whether I have slept. I am a different kind of mum depending on what is being asked of me.

Sometimes, I am an Exhausted Mum. On rare occasions, I am a Sweary Mum. Sometimes, I am a Patient Mum. Other times I am a 'WILL-YOU-PACK-IT-IN!' Mum. Sometimes, albeit infrequently, I am a Foodie Mum, cooking something from scratch and enjoying doing so. Other times, I am a Freezer Surprise Mum, digging deep into the drawers to pull together a Captain Birdseye meets Aunt Bessie feast with a token guilty side-helping of peas. Sometimes, I am a Fun Mum, tickling the boys until they are laughing so much they wee themselves. Sometimes, I am a Strict Mum, limiting TV time, rationing sugary snacks and generally ruining fun in the interest of their long-term wellbeing. Sometimes, I am a Good Mum. Other times, I am a Good Enough Mum. Yet whatever 'type' of mum I may be, and whatever day it is, as far as the kids are concerned, I'm just *their* mum. Nothing more, nothing less.

# Names

'Any names yet?'

You may not realise it, but your answer to this question will be a defining moment of your pregnancy adventure. You must pick a lane and stay in it. Do you remain politely guarded, keeping your name/s under your hat, revealing the chosen one only once the baby arrives? Or do you divulge your shortlist to friends and family, encouraging helpful (ahem) input and alternative suggestions?

I wish I could tell you we'd had the willpower to go with the under-our-hats approach, but I am terribly indiscreet – it's a challenge for me to keep someone else's secrets, let alone my own and, during every pregnancy, the moment someone else started talking about their baby-name ideas I found myself itching to blurt out our entire shortlist. All three times I ended up being an open book about our selection, and I do have regrets about that because, regardless of how much you *think* the opinions of others won't influence you, in practice, it's really hard to stop that from happening.

I have remarked in the past that opinions are like arseholes – everybody has one – and that's certainly true when it comes to baby-name opinions. In fact, I think those opinions might be the arseholiest of all. It *never* ceases to amaze me how forthcoming people are with their views on baby names and how willing they are to pooh-pooh name suggestions that you are seriously considering. I don't mind it quite so much from family – I had kidded myself that I didn't care what they thought when, in all honesty, I did care a little bit, so having a steer on which of our shortlisted names they preferred was helpful.

What is never helpful is when people take the time to suggest alternatives when you are not even in the market for alternatives. You could offer your Top Five, narrowed down over many months from an extensive longlist, and Julie from the office will say, 'Ah, but what about [insert name you've never mentioned which is probably horrific]?' No, Julie, that's not in the running.

When I was pregnant for the third time, 'Wilf' was a strong contender from the beginning, but I had a wobble in the middle of the pregnancy because it had also been on my shortlist for the other two. I wondered if it was wrong to call up a name that had been on the subs' bench for six years, and therefore set about finding an alternative, a new name that was his and his alone. At one stage, he was going to be Casper. This was closely followed by a Ned phase which actually endured for a few weeks – I do really love the name – until someone told me he'd never be able to go to Scotland.* When mooting the name Wilf as an option to someone I used to work with, she said, 'Are you sure you don't mean *Will?*', as though I'd made a spoken typo.

If I've learned anything at all when it comes to baby names, it's that you will never please all of the people all of the time and, if you can keep your choices under your hat, you're more likely to protect them. Not just from being tainted by others' opinions but also from being pinched – I know someone who divulged her top girl's-name choice (first name plus middle name) to a close work colleague, only for that colleague to announce her own pregnancy, give birth first and use both the first name and middle name for her baby, denying all knowledge of The Chat. Absolute scandal.

Generally, you will find that people will show more restraint and be slightly less direct with their criticism once the baby has arrived and you've announced it. They still don't have to love it, of course, but the chances of someone saying, 'God, no, that's terrible, what about Gary instead?' are slimmer. Whatever you do, don't ask for people's opinions unless you're genuinely prepared for them.

· · · · · · · · · · · · ·

* 'Ned' in Scotland is a derogatory term for yobs, hooligans or petty criminals. It's sometimes said to be an acronym for 'non-educated delinquent' and is basically the Scottish version of what we know to be 'chav'. I tried so hard to unlearn this piece of 'helpful' information, but it was no use, Ned Turner just wasn't going to happen after that.

# Nappy Changing

Five facts about nappies (and the changing thereof):

1. *Babies will lull you into a false sense of poo security, where you think you know their bowel routine. You do not know their bowel routine. Even if they 'poo like clockwork' six days out of seven, they will still manage to surprise everyone by doing an unscheduled explosion. This will be met with disbelief as you find yourselves saying, 'But he's only just done one!', moments after you've got him settled into a highchair in Pizza Express.*

2. Changing the nappy of a baby or toddler who doesn't want to have their nappy changed is like wrestling an angry octopus into a paper bag.

3. To combat the difficulties you face with the above wrestle, you will resort to doing silly faces, silly voices and high-pitched noises before placing the nearest object you can find in their hands to distract them while you get the old nappy off and the new nappy on. If you're lucky, small babies might be momentarily distracted by the rustle of the wipes packet or two pieces of Duplo they can bang together. Older babies will look at you in disgust until you give them the hard stuff, which includes but is not limited to: TV remotes, iPhones, PlayStation controllers, posh make-up brushes, car keys. Don't even think about offering them the pretend 'lights and sounds' car keys you bought. They want the real ones, so they can chew the key that has the battery in it.

4. The smell of your baby's dirty nappy, no matter how toxic, is still favourable to the smell of somebody else's baby's dirty nappy. Don't ask me why, maybe it's an evolutionary thing and we are programmed to somehow tolerate the smell better if it belongs to our own. This means that even when you walk into your living room post nappy-change and exclaim, 'Jesus Christ, it stinks in here!', you will still happily put the telly on and make yourself comfy amidst the fetid odour. Family is family.

5. At some stage, when you are potty training and suddenly faced with the prospect of free-range poo that is no longer contained inside a hammock, you will realise that nappies weren't so bad after all.

# The National Trust

There was great excitement in the Turner household the day our National Trust membership came through. It felt like a big moment. Finally, we had a sticker for our car windscreen that we hoped would convince our neighbours that we were a nice, respectable family. We feared they thought we were far from 'proper' after they'd witnessed two of our children opening the door to take delivery of a takeaway wearing nothing but wrestling masks at 5 p.m. on a Wednesday.

We'd toyed with the idea of signing up for a few years previously but had always decided against it. Firstly, it's not an insignificant spend – would we really get enough use out of our membership to justify why we weren't just plodding to the local park again? Secondly, and I think, deep down, this was the sticking point for me, a National Trust membership would confirm a long-held suspicion of mine: I was turning into my mother.

I have a vivid childhood memory of standing in the kitchen with my sister, who's a few years older than me and at the time wore mood-stone jewellery and decorated her entire bedroom with *Smash Hits* magazine stickers, waiting to find out our fate for the day ahead. It must have been a weekend morning and the *What shall we do today?* conversation had started. We'd thrown some ideas into the mix: swimming – preferably somewhere with flumes and rapids; ice-skating; a theme park; trampolining; the cinema ... the possibilities were endless! Mum and Dad had exchanged glances at our suggestions before announcing, with clapped hands, that we would save those activities 'for another day' because instead we were heading to Lanhydrock (a Victorian country house in Cornwall) *for a mooch around*. I can't remember exactly what happened next, but I imagine there was moaning, as there is not a lot pre-teen children enjoy about *mooching*, particularly when the mooch destination is basically just a big house with posh gardens where you're not allowed to touch anything.

Even more tragic for us on those National Trust days out was that Mum was the greatest ever advocate of the packed lunch. Whenever we were at those big houses with posh gardens, we would walk past the inviting aroma of soups and cakes wafting out of the tearooms – and then keep walking until we found a suitable bench or log to sit on and eat our home-made cheese sandwiches. 'There's no point *buying* food when we can bring food from home,' she would say as we sat and watched all the middle-aged people in Berghaus anoraks step out of the cold. 'Plus, their soups are extortionately priced. I can make one that'll last the four of us for a week for the same price!'

Twenty-something years later, and I get it now. The Sunday-morning indecision about where to go for the day, the little eyes pleading for some soft-play-hell labyrinth that smells of feet, the unwillingness to spend the best part of a hundred quid on theme-park tickets versus the familiar safety of the oak leaves signposting those big houses with posh gardens, entry to all of which you've already paid in advance for the year. Things have come on a lot since we were kids, too, and there seems to be so much more aimed at children – Easter Egg hunts, half-term challenges, decent play areas. So despite their initial reluctance to take their eyes off the television, our brood do love a good National Trust visit.

Although there are a great many parallels, I can't recall any occasion where my sister and I ran around the gardens of Lanhydrock shouting, 'No, *you're* a stinky butt-hole head!', which is exactly what my boys shouted at each other in the grounds of Killerton House a few weeks ago as James and I tried to explain that this was the National Trust, *you simply can't do that here.*

It was some time later, in the café queue, when I heard myself saying, '*Three pounds* for a kids' cheese sandwich! It's not even a whole sandwich, it's one piece of bread, folded in two! Three bloody pounds for half a sandwich!', that I knew once and for all that I had indeed become my mother. Packed lunches all round from now on.

# NCT

I'm unable to speak from personal experience when it comes to NCT (National Childbirth Trust) classes because when we were expecting our first baby we lived in the arse-end of nowhere with no class being offered nearby. Instead, we did the free antenatal evening sessions where we had to break off into groups and write down any burning questions we had about birth ('Will I poo when I push?') on a flipchart. No effort was made to 'bond' us as a group and, other than a quite-by-chance meeting with one of the other mums when she was putting her bins out one evening, I never saw any of the others again. There were biscuits, though, so it wasn't all bad.

I could, however, dedicate an entire book to stories other parents have told me about their NCT groups. I would call it *The Good, The Bad and The Weird Dads*. The Good would be all the times it has worked out beautifully, where genuine, long-lasting friendships have blossomed from the common ground that was essentially having had sex to conceive babies at a similar time. You can usually spot an NCT group photo a mile off because there'll be no sign of the parents and the kids will be lined up on a sofa looking confused. The same shot will be re-created every year until the kids start rolling their eyes (it gets to be a bit of a squeeze when they're fifteen). It's no exaggeration to say very best 'mum friends' have been made this way, and that's exactly why I had wanted to find a group local to me in the first place and why I was gutted when there wasn't one. I wanted a ready-made batch of pals for Henry, complete with parents I could bond with. I wanted a picture of him sat amongst his besties on the sofa. I felt cheated.

The Bad NCT stories I've been sent over the years have described the perhaps inevitable consequence of different people with very different ideas being flung together. The clenched teeth and tight smiles can only endure for so long before someone snaps and either the group fragments or a particularly difficult individual becomes ostracised. The worst such example I've heard where it's all turned a bit sour came from a mum who told me she'd despised one of the mums in her group from the word go but had tolerated 'being preached to and looked down on' for the benefit of the wider group. That was until one day when, after a heated exchange about cloth nappies in the middle of a coffee shop, she could bear it no more and left, saying, 'If she's staying, I'm going.' That evening, an invitation to join a new WhatsApp group for all members, excluding the one they deemed preachy, was received and, for the first time ever, plans were made for the original mum group minus its most difficult member to meet at the zoo, covertly. The mum who messaged me said they were having a great day and had almost forgotten about the missing member of their party … right up until the moment they walked around the corner from the penguin pool and bumped straight into her. Can. You. Imagine. The level of awkwardness here, for all involved, doesn't bear thinking about. It makes me want to hug the mum who they'd excluded, even though, by the sounds of it, she hadn't done herself any favours.

When it comes to Weird Dads, it was an old colleague of mine who first made me howl with laughter when he described the inaugural NCT group outing he'd been dragged to. He was under the impression that all the dads would be of the same mind, cursing the forced friendships that were being thrust upon them by their well-meaning other halves, who'd taken 'double dates' to a new level – a bleaker level, as there was now no alcohol. What he hadn't prepared for was Geoff,* dad to Finley and husband to Mandy, who behaved so much like David Brent that my mate initially thought he was taking the piss. As the group sat slightly awkwardly around the lunch table at one of the couples' houses, Geoff suggested that everyone 'introduce themselves with an interesting fact'. Assuming this was a wind-up, my pal laughed out loud, 'Good one, Geoff!', before seeing Geoff's brow furrow and promptly changing his laugh to a cough. On a separate occasion, Geoff turned up to the beach on a warm day wearing walking trousers teamed with a bumbag and, when he was asked what he kept in it, he replied simply, 'Lifesaving supplies.'

I also had a message from a mum who had persuaded her husband to join a mums-and-dads picnic outing to the park by promising him that everyone was 'normal'. As they debriefed much later in the day, he told her that he didn't want to make friends with people who had 'given up on life', something he was certain they had done because they were discussing seven-seater people carriers.

I'm therefore certain that, just like any method of friend-finding you have to sign up for, NCT appears to be a mixed bag. If I had my time again, I'd probably sign up purely in the hope of meeting a Geoff. I love a bumbag.

. . . . . . . . . . . . .

* Names have been changed to protect my friend from being sacked from his NCT group.

# O

## Off Days

I wonder what it is about parenting that turns us all into our own worst critics, more so than any other area of our lives?

When it comes to the other stuff, we generally forgive ourselves for having the odd 'off day'. The occasional unproductive day at work, when you have a list as long as your arm of tasks that need completing but somehow only get around to finishing a Facebook quiz to find out what your pornstar name would be.* Days when your mojo goes AWOL. Days

. . . . . . . . . . . .

* It's actually very simple. Just take the name of your first childhood pet followed by the first part of the street you grew up on. My pornstar name is Crumble Dunheved, which I'm not sure would attract many punters.

when you had one too many the night before. Days when you drop the ball and send an email slagging off Brian from Sales, to Brian from Sales.

In relationships, too, there are times we screw up. Forget to send a friend a birthday card. Do or say something hurtful to a partner in the heat of the moment and owe them an apology. Sometimes we feel bad about it for a while afterwards, but rarely do we allow ourselves to live under a cloud of remorse indefinitely. That's because we don't assume that those days are a fair reflection of our overall standard as an employee/friend/lover. We just had an off day. An off couple of days, perhaps. It happens.

When it comes to parenting, however, we rarely allow ourselves the same slack. Or indeed any slack: on those hurried mornings when we forget that it's Jeans for Genes day at nursery and arrive to a sea of denim and a sinking feeling. Or when, after enduring hour upon hour of sibling scrapping, something snaps and we end up shrieking like a fishwife in the park, before dragging the offending children home by their coat hoods under the judgemental glare of other parents. The better parents.

I know, or at least I do now, after having been unconvinced for a long while, that I am a good mum. Sometimes it feels good to say it. *I am a good mum.* (In my head or quietly to myself, I mean, not out loud at the school gates, as that might make me sound like a bit of a twat.) I do my best for my boys; they are safe, happy and loved beyond measure.

I also know that there are days when I am not such a good mum. When I'm exhausted or frustrated or a bit under the weather. When I'm preoccupied with work or just feeling a bit low. Sometimes I am all those things at once.

When that happens, it is hard not to beat yourself up and very easy to find yourself falling headfirst into an

I'm-not-good-enough vortex where you question your parental capabilities and say, 'I just can't do this today.' The thing I have come to realise about being a parent, however, is that you *do* do it. On those days when you don't think you can, when for whatever reason you're not firing on all parenting cylinders and are in desperate need of a break, you still show up.

So, no, your children might not always get the best of you, but that's only because the best of you isn't always there to give. And rather than those 'off days' signalling that you are a bad parent, maybe, just maybe, it's the giving of whatever you've got, when there is next to nothing left in the tank, that makes you a bloody good one.

# Old

Regardless of your age, having kids will make you feel old. The worst 'God, I'm old' moments for me, to date, have been as follows:

1. *Henry finding a cassette tape; me telling him that mix tapes were what we used to put our 'playlists' on in the olden days; and him proceeding to turn the tape over and over in his hands, searching for the headphones hole.*

2. *On a similar theme, the boys being confused when I asked James if he could 'tape' something for me off the telly. 'Taping' as a reference is completely lost on them.*

3. *Realising that some of the key workers at their nursery were born after 2000 yet can still legally look after my children and drink alcohol (not at the same time,*

*obviously, though I can't say I would blame them if they needed a quick swig).*

4. *Trying to explain to Henry how we chatted with friends 'back in the day' i.e. phoning a landline, after 6 p.m. (and having to hang up before the hour was up), and how the internet had a dial-up connection that took for ever and then cut out when the phone rang, ruining the flirting you were trying to do on MSN Messenger. He reacted to my story with such wonder I might as well have told him I'd survived the First World War.*

5. *Asking Jude how old he thought I was and him replying, 'Fifty?' Upon correcting him that I was, in fact, only thirty-one, he said, 'Still really old.' Cheers, bud.*

# 'Only a Phase'

This trusty adage will be offered liberally both by those you know and those you don't know the *moment* you complain about something.

Baby won't sleep? I wouldn't worry, it's only a phase.

Child having regular and violent meltdowns? Just a phase.

Toddler withholding their poo post potty-training? (Yes, this can happen.) A phase!

Whole house struggling to adapt to the new dynamic and really needing help or just reassurance that the soul-destroying crying and tiredness you're feeling doesn't mean you're – oh, what's that? It's

just a phase. Fab. Thanks, Barbara. Feel so much
better now.

Eye rolls aside, there is definitely some truth to the 'This,
too, shall pass' advice. You might want to punch Barbara in the
face but 'It's only a phase' comes from a good place. Usually,
from someone who has been through the phase themselves
and lived to tell the tale.

What they don't tell you is that each tricky parenting phase
rolls into the next one until you find yourself living in a perpet-
ual phase made up of overlapping phases. I suppose it's not
quite as catchy.

# Panic Priming

If you don't know what this means, you probably don't do it. If you're thinking it's something to do with make-up priming, it's not, though I do apply most of my make-up in a rushed panic so, arguably, it could work there, too. I am, of course, talking about Amazon Prime.

For me, panic Priming is never the intention but ends up being the trusty go-to when I find myself overhearing a conversation in the playground then saying, 'Fuck! Is that *this* Thursday?' before trotting home, trawling Amazon and committing to buy whatever's guaranteed to turn up the next day. There are no real excuses. I have usually been made aware in advance, via general chat or newsletters sent home, that particular events are coming up: someone's birthday, a dress-up or dress-down day at school or nursery – all things I could put on a calendar or set myself a reminder for in good time to get accessories, presents or props sorted. It's disorganisation and sometimes sheer idleness on my part that means I resort to making a rushed purchase at the eleventh hour.

On an ethical, social and environmental level, I am certainly not proud of the fact that I'm part of a 'worrying trend' of frenzied consumerism that my dad would tell you is 'everything that's wrong with the world today'. Generally speaking, I *have* been making more of an effort to support smaller, local businesses (or at least smaller businesses online), but I'd be lying to myself if I said I thought that buying the odd antique vase or cactus from an indie shop in town makes up for the sometimes thrice-weekly Amazoning executed in my PJs in front of *I'm a Celebrity*. I blame the Prime service for this – previously, if I knew something would have taken a couple of days to arrive, I would probably have popped to the shops (or a twenty-four-hour supermarket, which I'm not sure is any better in terms of panic consumerism). It's just too easy – the house could be falling down around me, and 'things to do' that haven't been done could be coming out of my ears, but I know that with a couple of clicks I can order a World Book Day costume and that it will be with me the next day. If that's wrong, I just don't think I've got the time to be right.

# Parklife

No longer just the title track from Blur's 1994 album, parklife takes on a different meaning as a parent. Less about cutting down on your porklife, mate, and getting some exercise, parent parklife simply refers to the number of hours you'll spend in the park (though, incidentally, this does result in you getting some exercise). Yes, if you have children, the chances are, you will have become a parkgoer.

The park can be your friend or your foe, depending on a number of factors. Chiefly: what the weather's doing, where your children are on the mood scale (from amenable to savage) and whether it's a decent park or a naff one. I rate my parks based on their proximity to the house, whether they have a toilet (or are near somewhere that does have a toilet) and what they offer both in terms of play equipment and green spaces for running around. Points are deducted for green spaces that are easily escapable, climbing frames that have been designed by sadists who enjoy seeing toddlers drop off the edge and the likelihood of encountering teenagers who will call each other 'c**t' a lot in earshot of the swings. The latter can sadly ruin an otherwise perfectly good park trip, which is not, of course, the park's fault, but trying to ignore conversations about giving head and getting wankered is hard when you're accompanied by children who repeat everything they hear, like antisocial parrots. It's also hard to explain to a four-year-old what the 'funny smell' wafting over the roundabout is.

On a good day, the park provides fresh air, exercise and a generous dose of fun. I've likened having boys to having dogs several times since becoming a mum and now that I've got three of the buggers I stand by that even more – they need a good run and a good meal before they'll settle down, so the park is our standard go-to for that. In our trillion and one park trips (to date) we've had some cracking fun: games of hide-and-seek, pretending to hunt for the Gruffalo, and there was even one occasion when I took a tartan blanket and we sat and ate sandwiches I'd packed in a mini cool-bag, which made me feel like something from a lifestyle-magazine shoot.

On a bad day, the park is cold, wet and windy and the kids behave like beasts for the entire trip. Some of the most embarrassing parenting moments I've been through have been park-based, including the time Henry did a 'quick wee' in a hedge that turned out to be a poo, the time Wilf screamed so loudly and incessantly that passers-by came to check on his wellbeing and the time Jude ran off to hang out with a group of shirtless men who were drinking tinnies at 3 p.m.

P

I once tried to be a fun football-playing mum in the park but went arse over tit when I kicked the ball and slipped, ending up really hurting my coccyx while other parents pretended not to be staring. As I hobbled home, Henry chuckled about how it was 'like something you see on the Falling Over programme!' (*You've Been Framed*).

One thing's for certain, like them or loathe them, parks are a parenting staple. An institution. Parklife is just part of life now.

# Playing Games

There are a great many things I enjoy doing with my kids. Reading to them, taking them to the theatre or to the beach. Just chatting to them is very often a pleasure, hearing their unique and at times a little off-the-wall take on the world around them. One thing I have always struggled to enjoy, however – and believe me, I feel bad for saying so – is playing games with them. I don't much enjoy that at all. If you're judging me at this point, perhaps thinking that I am not cherishing the time I have with my children in the way I ought to be, then I'm afraid you are mistaken. It's not my fault, you see. It's theirs. A classic case of *it's not me, it's them*. They are a fucking nightmare to play games with.

It was bad enough when Henry and Jude were toddlers. They weren't toddlers at the same time, of course, but Jude's toddlerhood closely followed Henry's, which meant we had a solid and extended block of toddler years to revel in. We're now about to extend this again, as Wilf is not far off entering the toddler stage. Playing together during this period mostly saw me playing a game that I could never win, or playing something so repetitive

153

that it made my brain shut down. The worst offender from Jude was 'playing trains', which *sounded* fun – I was all up for helping him build a track, etc. – but as soon as I had built a track with tunnels and crossings and little children standing at the station, he would declare that he didn't want the trains to be *on* the track and instead wanted to push his train around on the floor with my train following his train at all times. This resulted in the pair of us pushing tiny Brio trains around the house, on our hands and knees, while 'choo'-ing. As an adult with creaky knees, there is only a limited amount of joy that can be gleaned from this. I would jump up with relief every time there was a knock at the door or my phone rang. I always knew the respite would be short-lived, though, and that as soon as I'd finished talking to the postman or signing for a parcel, Jude would look up at me and say, 'Are we playing trains again now? This one's yours,' as he handed me whichever train was the most crap and summoned me to the ground again.

There was, at least, a pureness to those games. There wasn't a hidden agenda and any cheating was so brazen that they could get away with it. A two-year-old whose bottom lip wobbles because you're beating him at a game is kind of cute. I should just let him win, I told myself, he's got his whole life to learn about losing.

Fast-forward to playing games with a seven-year-old and a four-year-old, and I can tell you that those bottom-lip wobbles, now accompanied by foot-stomping and storming out of the room, are much less cute. In fact, playing games with Henry and Jude is probably one of the most frustrating (current) parts of being a parent, all the more frustrating because I keep hoping that this time will be different, *it will be fun*, and of course it isn't. If you're still judging me from this admission, I'd like to run you through how every game I play with the boys pans out.

Henry is now mad keen on football. He goes to football club after school on a Thursday and this means he is always eager to show off his skills. Whereas a toddler Henry would have guilt-tripped me into letting him score the winning goal, he now thinks he is Mo Salah and, as such, doesn't need me to let him win. He will win on his own merit, which he does by pushing me out of the way when I have got the ball (not a foul; only a foul if I do it) and subtly changing the rules as we go. There are some surprising changes to the official rules of football in 2019, if Henry is telling me the truth, which I am *sure* he is. Penalty shoot-outs are certainly a lot more fluid than I remember them being. Admittedly, my football knowledge is based almost entirely on dipping into the World Cup and having Sky Sports News on at the weekends, but I can't recall seeing or hearing about a game where it was 'best of six' because Liverpool started crying when they weren't ahead after best of five. We got to 'best of eleven' recently, and even then the sudden-death penalties that followed were shady because Henry 'slipped' on thin air, which made him miss and therefore entitled him to another go.

Lego is something I would happily spend hours building with the boys. I get quite into whatever I'm creating and find it almost meditative. When playing Lego with Jude, however, he is adamant that all the time I spend building Lego while sitting cross-legged next to him on the floor of his bedroom 'doesn't count as playing'. *Playing* Lego means I must have a Lego character (one that he decides I can have, which, yep, you guessed it, will be whichever one is the most crap) and then act out a little scene where my character interacts with his full cast of characters. I'd hoped this would be more fun after we bought him the Harry Potter Hogwarts Lego set for Christmas. However, any attempts to steer our game towards logical Harry Potter storylines – Harry, Ron and Hermione off on an adventure, the kids all finding out their fate from the Sorting Hat, that sort of thing – are shunned by Jude, who insists on mixing up all his toys (shudder) and instead wants to play the lesser-known 'Ron Weasley gets attacked by a Ninja Turtle then saved by Braun Strowman', which takes place outside the grounds of Hogwarts in his WWE ring. I'm only ever allowed to be Professor Quirrell.

Perhaps worse than either of the above is playing card games or board games. There's probably no need for me to outline the sequence of events that unfolds when we crack those bad boys out, but let's just say it always ends up with at least one child crying and me having to excuse myself to calm down a bit, before the urge to shout, 'Stop cheating, you morons!' gets the better of me.

So, you can judge me all you like, but when my children say, 'Mummy, will you play a game with me?' a small piece of me dies inside. Wilf might be different, of course. He might play with grace as a toddler then grow up to play a proper Harry Potter Lego role-play with me where I'm allowed to be Hermione. Come on, Wilf, don't let me down.

# Postpartum

I found a lot of the stuff that happened to me postpartum, first time around, quite surprising. Maybe that's because I'd focused so much of my time and energy on the pregnancy and birth, on growing and delivering the baby safely, that I'd had little regard for what would happen next. I'm sure that in those pregnancy guides you buy – the ones where on the cover a radiant mum-to-be is wearing white and smiling like she's just heard the best joke from the Edinburgh Fringe – there are sections with useful information about what happens post-birth. I probably just stopped reading after I'd reached the bit about crowning – a friend of a friend described crowning as 'the ring of fire' and I just didn't feel like I needed to know much beyond that – if we'd made it that far, I'd surely work out the rest?

It was a surprise to me, therefore, that the placenta didn't come out at exactly the same time as the baby. I fear this might make you think I'm stupid and, if so, so be it, but I just didn't know. I thought it would just kind of plop out in the baby's slipstream and was most aggrieved to discover I actually had to deliver it. I also didn't know that said placenta could get stuck, which happened to me with babies two and three. Clearly, I should at least have read the placenta chapter.

Another surprise was the duration of the postpartum bleeding and all the fun that brought with it (see Vagina for the full surprise story there; thank me later). I think I *had* read somewhere that it could be very heavy initially and that it might last a couple of months, but I'd assumed that was an error – it just seemed remarkable that someone could bleed for sixty days and not die.

I'd also not realised that you get 'after pains' or cramps after delivery, caused by your uterus contracting to its normal size after pregnancy, nor that breastfeeding could make the cramps stronger (the baby feeding triggers the release of oxytocin, which in turn triggers contractions, I think the midwife said). A couple of the cramps soon after Henry was born were so intense I was convinced there was another baby in there, a twin that must have been hiding behind him at all the scans.

Then there was the postpartum hair loss. Holy Mother of God, I thought I was going bald. My hair was *everywhere*. All over my clothes, in the shower, in our dinners. I would run my hand through it and clumps would fall out; it was, quite honestly, horrific. My hairdresser explained to me that, ordinarily, we lose hair every day but that during pregnancy, because of hormonal changes, that part of the typical hair cycle kind of freezes – in other words, hair that would usually fall out doesn't. After you've given birth, all the hair that stayed put then starts to fall out, which looks more alarming than it is. I'm sure my hairdresser was right but I never felt the benefit of thicker hair during pregnancy and more than a year after the third baby I'm still finding fur balls everywhere, so I can't help but think that my oestrogen levels have gone to shit somewhere along the line.

On reflection, perhaps it's not such a bad thing that I skipped the postpartum section of the guidebooks. Much more fun to just let it play out.

# Potty Training

'Do you need a wee?'

'Do you need a wee yet?'

'Tell Mummy when you need a wee, OK?'

'Do you want to just try for a wee?'

'How about now?'

'Do you need … oh. Oh dear. Whoopsie daisy, never mind. It doesn't matter. Let's get you changed.'

The most difficult thing for us when it came to potty training Henry and Jude (we've still got it all to come with Wilf, which is precisely why we are not yet putting in any new carpets downstairs in the house we recently bought) was getting the boys to sense the difference between a nappy and their pants. Aside from the as-to-be-expected early mishaps, we found they were really good at using the potty or the toilet, just as long as we were at home and they were naked. With Jude, his potty use when naked from the waist down was so impressive I thought we'd cracked the whole thing in about twenty-four hours. Then I put pants on him and he indiscriminately pissed everywhere. I'm guessing there's probably something clever we didn't do that we ought to have done to encourage the progression from naked to pant-wearing without it resulting in everything getting saturated, but we muddled along just fine and they got there in the end.

That said, we did lose a rug in the process, and there was one time I found myself clearing up the aftermath of a number two from the floor of the car after my newly 'potty-trained' child forgot to tell me he'd let one escape and it dropped out of the bottom of his shorts when he climbed out. I've never been so grateful to see a solid poo.

# PTA

All hail the PTA! Or the PTFA (Parents Teachers and Friends Association), if you're being friendly. I'm not taking the piss, either.

It's true, I have been known to have the odd moan about the volume of gentle reminders to buy / sell raffle tickets, closely followed by reminders that I am also expected to contribute hamper goods to said raffle. I may at times avoid eye contact with key members of the PTA Massive, certain they know I have never once made cakes for the 'Friday Feast'. I have probably even been guilty, in the past, of looking at those who willingly dedicate so much of their spare time to organising Christmas Fayres a little suspiciously.

Yet I have realised that, when it comes down to it, without the PTA, no shit would get done. There would be no school disco, no cakes, no fundraising, no fayres, and then we really would have something to complain about.

# P

If you're on the PTA at your school, you are a good person. Grumpy parents like me who leave it all to you really *do* appreciate your efforts. We're just acting shifty because we're worried you're going to ask us to volunteer for something.

# Queuing

Avoid queues at all costs, from now until your children have left home. Kids simply cannot cope with queuing. Exceptions (i.e. when you have no choice) include airport check-ins and queues for rides at various UK attractions where you will all feel faint and be stung by wasps. Whether those exceptions are worth the hassle or not is your call, but they are, at least, big events. If you find yourself out shopping and in a queue with more than ten people ahead of you, abandon the basket and leave immediately. If you have more than one child with you, reduce the ten-person ceiling to five. Go home.

# Quiet

I can just about remember what quiet sounds like. Or rather, I can remember what it doesn't sound like.

It doesn't sound like a high-pitched animation of 'Baby Shark (Doo Doo Doo Doo Doo Doo)'.

It doesn't sound like a fight breaking out over whose turn it is to play with the light saber.

It doesn't sound like the constant static of a walkie-talkie that has been left on but which nobody can find.

It doesn't sound like a million and one questions starting 'Mum ...' before you've even made it out of bed.

It doesn't sound like a loud bang from upstairs that you fear was someone falling off a bed, followed by a piercing cry which confirms it was indeed someone falling off a bed.

It doesn't sound like annoying musical toys that won't die even when you take the batteries out.

It doesn't sound like whingeing, or squabbles in the car, or Mario Kart, or farting.

When we do now get a moment of quiet as parents, which is rare but does happen occasionally, it is almost too much of a shock for our brains to process. Even the standard designated 'quiet time' we look forward to when all the kids are asleep sees us walking around to the background drone of an 'industrial fan' because Wilf has slept with a white-noise machine in his room since he was around three months old. (I know, I know, rod for our own backs.)

# Q

The last time I found myself enjoying a moment of total quiet – I think the kids had gone out for a walk with Granny and Grandad – I finally appreciated the phrase, 'It's so loud, I can't hear myself think!', because, all of a sudden, I *could* hear myself think and it was almost deafening. The quietness felt so alien that the thoughts in my head seemed so loud! It was as though my head-voice was shouting but, of course, she wasn't shouting, I was just used to her being drowned out by the noise of kids.

Though I joke about never 'getting any peace or bloody quiet', I *do* think the chaos and the noise is something I will miss one day. I'm sure, someday, I'll be sat in an empty house, in silence, when the boys have gone off to university, or moved to Singapore, or are in the honeymoon period with a girlfriend or boyfriend and don't have time to visit their old mum, and the quiet will make me a bit sad. So, for the time being, I'm going to embrace the fact that peace and quiet is just not the life stage we are at right now.

I'm also going to try and phase out Wilf's white-noise machine because, as happy as I have always been to make a rod for my own back (if it's a rod that works), writing about our family's reliance on a fan noise at night-time has made me realise it is a bit ridiculous.

# Regression

You must never say, 'My baby sleeps through,' out loud; or if you do, you must prefix it with, 'It's probably just a fluke,' or 'We've been lucky so far.' Failure to do so means you will almost certainly have done something you will live to regret: spoken too soon.

Speaking too soon is an easy trap to fall into as a parent. At a time when you've become obsessed with sleep – how much the baby's had, how much next-door's baby has had, how much you've not had – it's only natural to want to celebrate the victories. The problem is, there's usually a plot twist on the horizon. What follows is a lot of disbelief and head-scratching as your previously sleep-reliable infant starts waking at 11 p.m. and 2 a.m. again, as they did in the newborn days, sometimes at midnight and 4 a.m., too, ready to party. Being awake several times during the night with a baby or toddler who is suddenly not tired, just when you thought you'd cracked it, feels even more brutal somehow than when they simply wouldn't sleep to begin with. *Now*, you have had a taste of what the good life feels like. For a few consecutive nights, you banked a decent block of uninterrupted sleep and felt the under-eye bags start to lift. Your brain became less foggy. It was all getting a bit easier, because everything is easier when you've caught up on sleep ... yet here you are, back to where you flipping started, standing on the landing in your pyjamas at midnight, your eyes half shut as you frantically attempt to 'Sssshhhh' the baby back towards slumber.

A quick search online tells you that this is a sleep 'regression' and that it's very common. You feel comforted by the fact there is a name for it – this means there must be a logical cause and, presumably, a fix to be found! However, after rooting around a bit further, you start to become suspicious. There's a lot of talk about the four-month sleep regression – that seems to be the biggie, so maybe that one's legit, but your baby is not four months old so you search instead for six-month sleep regression, or twelve-month sleep regression, or fourteen-and-three-quarters-month sleep regression and find that someone, somewhere, has previously searched for every age going. The regression appears to be birth to age fifteen, so you quit browsing and decide instead that tomorrow will be different. This was just a blip. You are not going back there. Hell to the no.

Other regressions include:

- *The daytime-nap regression, which is closely linked and occurs when a previously nap-happy baby goes on strike. At some point you will realise that the worst has happened and the nap has been dropped permanently – this is a very sad day indeed.*

- *The potty-training regression, where a toddler who had been otherwise successfully using the potty or toilet for months starts to forget to listen to their bodily cues. This may result in you standing beneath a play enclosure at Crealy Adventure Park wondering why your child is waddling out to you wearing a look of panic and, worse, wondering how the bloody hell you're going to deal with the aftermath of whatever's happened, as you've been stupid enough to leave the house without spares or baby wipes. True story, unfortunately. I was able to salvage the trousers, threw the pooey pants in the bin and 'flannel-washed' the child in question using soap from the soap dispenser, warm water and my jumper, which I then bagged up and took home, as though I had soiled myself.*

- *The food regression, where all the things they did like become all the things they don't. They will now only eat dry cereal again.*

In fact, there is probably a regression for everything, and I certainly like to milk it as an excuse for anything my children are doing, or not doing. 'What's that? He's been sticking his tongue out at everyone on the bus while singing "Na na na na na"? I do apologise, it's the twenty-four-and-a-bit-month behaviour regression. Hopefully, it'll pass soon.'

# Repetition

There is an awful lot about parenting that is repetitive. Sometimes, that repetition is useful. Comforting, even (see Routine).

However, it is very easy, and perfectly normal, to grow tired of doing the same things over and over again, day in, day out, and the worst such monotony offender is hearing yourself *saying* the same things, on a loop, until you'd be happy never to hear yourself talking again.

I've often thought I should just record myself saying a series of stock expressions as a sort of 'nagging' playlist, with tracks queued up to play depending on what time of day it is. That way, I wouldn't have to actively repeat myself. I could just go out and leave the kids to it. I'll get to work on producing a recording of the below and let you know when it's ready to download. Or 'stream', as the kids say.

1. *Will You Pack It In?*

2. *Yes, I Said in a Minute*

3. *Why Are You Shouting?*

4. *Has Anyone Seen the TV Remote?*

5. *Ssssshhh*

6. *Leave Your Willy Alone*

7. *Stop Moaning*

8. *Does This Look Tidy to You?*

9. *We All Need to Calm Down a Bit*

10. *Please Just Do as I Ask*

# Routine

Have you got one? Do you need one? What even is one? In general terms, a routine is a sequence of actions that are regularly followed. In parenting terms, a routine is what stops your mate coming out for lunch because it interferes with her baby's nap time, snack time, song time or quiet time.

Since producing a third child, I have shifted my thoughts on having a routine, and it's probably not shifted in the direction you might assume. As a rule, people think you start off anal about getting your baby into a routine and then, the more kids you have, the more chilled you become and, therefore, the more your routine goes to pot. I have learned, however, that while there probably is some truth to the mellowing over time (and subsequent babies) thing – heaven knows, my standards are slacker overall, three children later! – whether or not you favour a strict or a lax routine depends largely on what sort of baby you get from the baby lottery. Yes, the parenting manuals will tell you that getting a baby into a routine rests with you, that their sleep behaviours rest with you and that, ultimately, a calm, contented, routine-conforming baby is the product of his or her parents' coaching, but I'm here to tell you that, sometimes, you just get a rogue one.

That's not to say that all the hard work parents put into establishing a routine should be undervalued – in many cases, that commitment really does pay off. I'm just saying that some babies are untrainable, even if Supernanny says they're not. I know this because we have tried to get all three of our babies into a consistent nap routine, and only two of them heeded the call.

Our first baby, the original pride and joy, Henry, was a daytime-nap refuser, in spite of our having the capacity to dedicate more time to enforce the nap. *We did all of the things.* We absorbed 'sleep training' advice like desperate sponges. We trialled different times of day for the nap. We left him to cry it out like a child from an NSPCC advert. We hated the crying so we lay next to him singing, 'Daisy, Daisy, give me your answer do.' We tried a little massage before nap time. We spritzed lavender sleep spray around the room to create positive sleep associations and we prayed to a God we didn't believe in. He would not nap.

This left me irritated by all the other parents I knew who had established uncompromising routines for their little ones. In part, I was irritated because I was jealous, and every time someone said anything about plans needing to fit in with nap time, it was like a dagger to the heart, reminding me of what we could have won (and what we hadn't achieved). Yet I was also irritated because, slowly but surely, a new routine was carved out for Henry and me based around the nap schedules of our friends' babies. Lunch on Wednesday had to be an early lunch because my friend's little boy liked a nap at 2 p.m. Coffee at the library on a Friday had to be at 9.30 a.m. so my other friend's little girl could have her nap late morning. They were being ridiculous by being so inflexible with their schedules, surely? I wanted to be difficult in return and say, 'Yeah, well, we can't do those times because of *our* routine!', but of course that would only have served to leave us friendless for coffees and lunches.

With Jude and Wilf, however, the routine penny dropped. Wilf, in particular, loves a morning nap. *Loves* it. At around 9.30 a.m. he starts rubbing his eyes, sucking his thumb and whinge-ing over nothing. He wants to go to bed. There is no singing, no lavender-spraying and rarely any crying-it-out (if there is, we've learned it's because he's just cross he's not yet asleep). We put him down for a nap and he naps. HE NAPS! Very occasionally, he decides a nap is off the agenda but 99 per cent of the time he will nap. It's beautiful. What this has meant, in terms of arranging catch-ups and coffee dates, is that I now fully understand the dread of being asked to go somewhere between 10 and 11.30 a.m. A mid-morning playdate is problematic for us because a) he'll be tired and testy without the nap, which will ruin everyone's experience and b) I'll miss out on the Golden Hour where he sleeps and I can have a cup of tea/play with his brothers without worrying he's sticking his fingers in plug sockets. I have become someone who says, 'Can we make it a bit later? It's just his nap time, you know how it is!'

If they *do* know how it is, they will be understanding.

If they don't know how it is, you should be understanding. Their baby is a nap-refuser and your thoughts should be with them at this difficult time.

# Safe Space

'Good as gold? Really?' I was picking Jude up from the child-minder at the end of a week when he had been anything but 'good as gold' at home. There had been tantrums. Some biting. An episode with a full potty and a TV remote. It seemed to me that either he was being Jekyll for the childminder and Hyde at home or our childminder was lying, and I didn't for one moment think it was the latter. Having previously experienced a very similar behaviour discrepancy between home and not-home (particularly nursery) with his big brother, I suspected it was simply the case that Jude was saving all his 'acting up' for home. Lucky us, eh?

What I have come to realise, however, is that although it can be infuriating to hear that your child has been behaving rationally and reasonably for others when they behave like an animal at home, it is actually, possibly, a good sign.

It's not an indication that they have zero respect for you, nor that their key worker from nursery has done a better job of enforcing boundaries than you have at home (though, in our case, that remains a possibility). Instead, their tendency to let rip at home is a sign that you represent their safe space. They play the fool at home because they are comfortable there. When Henry gets home from school, after 'working hard' all day, it feels like a switch has been flipped. He strops about, moans, tells us his life is unfair, and then we sit there scratching our heads, wondering how it's possible for our 'sensible' schoolchild to turn into a bit of a moron as soon as he's back at home.

He's tired, he tells us, particularly when the end of term rolls around, and I am sure that is true. I am also sure that he doesn't skip out of the classroom at the end of the day intending to misbehave or grumble all evening, but his guard drops at home and, as a result, he stops making so much of an effort. It's as though the control he's maintained throughout the day goes to pot when he's back at home and maybe that's not because he hates us and we're crap at discipline but rather because he knows we are always there. We are his constant. He doesn't feel the need to impress us or make us like him, and he's not worried about making sense of a maths problem so we'll think he's clever. He is relaxed and at ease at home and, because of that, we sometimes get the worst of him.

I'm not sure that entirely negates the pain of being the punching bag or the whinge-receiver, and it would certainly be nice if the sensible, hard-working schoolchild and his 'absolutely delightful' younger brothers could stay in role at home, too, but I understand at least a little bit why they don't. They can't be on top form 100 per cent of the time and, if shit is going to get real, I suppose I would rather it got real with us than anywhere else. I just wish us parents had a safe space, too. There's always the pub, I suppose.

# Screen Time

Kids today are spending far too many hours in a zombified state staring blankly at television screens and iPads or, worse, sitting in their bedrooms in front of a computer game trying to scavenge supplies to survive inside a virtual world. This is very bad indeed. We ought to be gravely concerned about the damaging effect that screen time is having on our children because it is ruining an entire generation and, if we don't act fast, our children will grow up to be emotionally fragile, unemployed and fat. Shit.

It is, of course, only sensible to heed warnings about the negative impact such pastimes can have, but I hope I speak for most parents when I say we don't need to read the findings from another new study to know that exposing our kids to hour upon hour of screen time is far from ideal – it's surely intuitive that endless hours of cartoons and video games cannot be healthy. What it doesn't seem sensible to do is panic, or put ourselves under unnecessary pressure to cut out screen time altogether. Why? Well, because for many of us, getting rid of screen time would be both unrealistic and unwise. Rightly or wrongly, we rely on it. It is how we get stuff done. If it makes me a bad parent to admit that I sometimes use CBeebies as a babysitter, then sue me – there are days when it feels like I'm practically co-parenting with Andy Day (unrelated to the dream I once had where he took me on a different kind of wild adventure) and while that might not be a desirable state of affairs, it's the real one.

Am I proud of the fact that Jude has watched so much *Peppa Pig* he can recite the episodes? No. Am I proud of the fact that *I* have watched so much *Peppa Pig* I am able to select my favourite episodes ('Mr Skinnylegs', Season 1; 'Compost', Season 3) and skip the episodes that make me groan (The Time Capsule', Season 2, 'Baby Alexander', Season 3)? No. In truth, I guessed it was probably time to start easing off the Peppathons when I found myself trying to talk to other adults about what I perceived to be the darker plot themes, most notably the controlling, belittling and blatant 'gaslighting' Daddy Pig suffers at the hands of Mummy Pig, who constantly puts him down and makes him feel useless.

Did I ever imagine I would allow Henry to get in from school, collapse on the sofa and play *Minecraft* on his Nintendo or *FIFA* on the PlayStation until teatime? Absolutely not. I imagined he would come home from school and sit at the table with a glass of milk and a plate of cookies I'd baked earlier in the day, working on some sums or perhaps reading a book aloud while I busied myself tidying an already spotless home before joining him at the table to marvel at his understanding of split digraphs (if you've not yet reached the school years, *everything* has changed: prepare to feel very stupid).

While a 'perfect' day for us might involve packing up a picnic and heading to Dartmoor to eat our sandwiches in close proximity to the ponies before dipping our toes in the river, there are many more days when there are no picnics (unless a 'snacky tea' on the rug in the living room counts), when fresh air comes from the seven-minute walk to school and the kids watch back-to-back Nickelodeon cartoons while I try to make a dent in the endless piles of washing created by a refluxy baby whose favourite food is spaghetti Bolognese and his brothers,

S

who put clean clothes on just to slide-tackle each other in the garden.

I know there are people, particularly those of a certain generation – many of whom I have spoken to at bus stops or in the supermarket – who believe that us millennials are 'making excuses' for our lazy parenting when, really, there can be no excuse for letting children fester indoors playing video games. 'Kids should be playing outside on their bikes,' they say. 'We never had iPads in my day.' I tend to smile and join in with the memory-lane trips about 'the good old days' because it feels less hassle in that moment than saying, 'But times have changed, so piss off.' The truth is, times *have* changed. By the time I was nine, twenty-something years ago, I was walking to and from school on my own with the front-door key around my neck on a shoelace, because both my mum and dad were at work from eight until after five. When they had stuff to do around the house, I wasn't 'babysat' by the telly, because there was no need – it was deemed perfectly safe for me to play with other kids who lived on our street and would knock for me and my sister before we all headed down to the garages that ran along the bottom of our gardens to do nothing in particular. It was the opposite of helicopter parenting. We probably had to be back by a certain time, we weren't allowed out when it was dark and we never strayed too far from the house, but there was still a great amount of unsupervised outdoor play going on.

Nowadays, that just wouldn't happen. Granted, Henry and Jude are both still quite young, but even if they were eleven and eight I can't imagine bundling them out of the door to play with friends who had knocked for them. I know we live in Exeter, which is hardly the ghetto, but there are dangers wherever you live, and I just wouldn't feel happy with them being out of my sight. In fact, just last year James was walking Jude back from nursery when he stumbled across three drug addicts crouched down, heating spoons, needles at the ready, poised to shoot up in the alleyway behind our back fence. Perhaps that's what I should say to 'in my day' comments at the bus stop next time, that yes, sometimes, I probably *do* make excuses for my boys' higher-than-ideal screen-time hours but I like to think that my preference for them watching repeats of *Scooby Doo* rather than gaining an introduction to tourniquets is an understandable one.

If you can set boundaries or limits on the time your kids spend in front of screens, then that's fabulous, a worthy exercise, but don't beat yourself up for relying on the odd hour (or three) of *Mario Kart* or *Ben and Holly's Little Kingdom* to help get stuff done once in a while. *Everything in moderation*, as they say, and we all know 'moderation' is a grey area.

# Separation Anxiety

I was first introduced to the term 'separation anxiety' when studying psychology in the sixth form. I can't fully remember the context, but it was something to do with the development of attachment in children and I can remember thinking it was terrible that, at the heart of it, babies and toddlers cry because they don't realise that when Mummy or Daddy go off to work for the day, they *will* be coming back. At some stage, of course, they learn that Mummy or Daddy being out of sight doesn't mean that they are gone for ever, but until then they have no way of knowing that the daily goodbye isn't a permanent farewell. How heartbreaking is that?

When I had kids, therefore, I guessed that separation anxiety would kick in at some point and imagined that, when it did, it would be one of the hardest parts of the whole parenting

S

experience. Indeed it did, and indeed it has, *but* it hasn't always been hard in quite the way I'd anticipated. Instead, it has presented a challenge on two levels.

The first has been the sort of separation anxiety I was expecting: the big separation stuff, the going-back-to-work-after-months-off stuff, the first-time-somebody-else-puts-the-baby-to-bed stuff, the starting-nursery stuff. I'd be lying if I said I had greatly enjoyed maternity leave – that's partly why I opted to go back to work after six months 'off' the first two times (and the third time handed the entire parental-leave baton over to my husband) – yet, regardless of whether or not you willingly go back to work, it is a huge emotional upheaval when you do. You will come to realise the separation anxiety exists on both sides. When I drove into work on my first day back after having Henry, having kissed him on the head and told him I'd see him a bit later, I actually felt quite ill. (I should add that he was left in the capable hands of my dad and not to his own devices with a packet of rice cakes in front of Baby TV.) When you're used to spending every moment of every day with someone, even if that someone has driven you to the brink of despair on several occasions, the attachment and bond you develop is intense. I drove away from him that morning thinking it felt *wrong*, worrying that he would be missing me and, even worse than that, remembering that bloody psychology lesson, which meant I was certain my little Henry would be convinced his mother had abandoned him for good.

When they first start at nursery or with a childminder and you're forced to gently prise off the little hands that are clinging to you and hand them over, it is just dreadful, and it doesn't really matter how many people tell you, 'Oh, he'll be fine!', because *you* are not fine. Separation anxiety in those moments is a killer.

The more surprising level of separation anxiety, the one no amount of AS level psychology can adequately prepare you for, is the demanding phase that occurs when your baby cannot bear to be separated from you even for a *second*. Forget worrying about exiting the house for work and start worrying about exiting the living room to grab the wet wipes – you will no longer be able to do anything without taking the baby with you, and I mean *anything*. Don't even think about putting them down or losing eye contact. We like to call this the 'Velcro baby' phase and, holy macaroni, it's a test. It seems to step up a gear somewhere between six and eighteen months, though it feels like our boys have experienced being 'anxiously separated' to varying degrees of extremity. With both Henry and Wilf, this stage has been arduous, to say the least, with Jude providing some respite in the middle – though I should point out that everything I've read suggests that separation anxiety is perfectly normal, so I am wondering whether Jude was less anxious because he was less attached to us?! (The joy of Parentland, where even the wins feel like losing!)

Before I had kids, I probably wouldn't have thought it would be a problem to have a child who wanted to be with me 24/7. I know there are lots of parents, perhaps those who favour the attachment parenting approach, or maybe just those who are more patient than I am, who wouldn't ever describe their baby or toddler as 'clingy'. They simply have a need to be close, they feel anxious when they are not close to you and the best thing you can do is just keep them bloody close to you. It sounds so simple. The problem comes when you try that approach but soon come to realise that having another human unremittingly strapped to your person, sometimes literally, is just not a practical way to live.

I love my boys. I would walk to the ends of the earth in flip-flops that are giving me toe blisters for them. I would jump in front of a lorry that was careering towards us to push them out of its path. I might even watch *Nativity 3* without looking at my phone for them, and we all know *Nativity* lost its way after #2. However, sometimes, I just need to know where I end and my children begin. I prefer weeing alone, without a toddler using my mid-wee knees as some kind of standing frame or trying to get involved when I'm changing a tampon. I like to be able to leave one room to pop quickly to the next without having to do a cheery song and dance to remind my distraught infant that I am not deserting him for ever. Which, of course, brings me right back to those psychology lessons and the knowledge I have deep down that when I leave Wilf in his high chair in the kitchen to pop to the living room to get his beaker, as far as he's concerned, I've left him for good. Sigh.

On reflection, I think it's a phase we just have to ride out. I'll keep doing whatever I can to reassure the buggers that when I strap them in their car seats and shut the car door I really am only going around to the front of the car to get in. As tempting as it has felt on the odd occasion to shut the door and keep walking, past the car and to the pub, or to the seaside, or anywhere I can exist in a 50cm radius of independence, I never have. Instead, I get in the car and reach back at an awkward angle to hold a tiny hand and remind my crying child that I am there. *Mummy's here.* Can she have her hand back now, though, or she can't drive to Tesco.

# Sharenting

Sharing is caring, or so they say, yet when it comes to parenting, ours is a generation of over-sharers. We are *sharents*. Social media has catapulted us into an age of ultra-divulgence where, even if we've decided against disclosing our every park trip, our every weaning woe, our every night-feed update, there's still a good chance we'll be consuming somebody else's through our phone screens.

Which begs the question, do we now know *too* much about each other? If I really stop and think about it, the thing that's most staggering – and this isn't me being disparaging in any way, because I am without doubt a 'sharent' myself! – is the scale of insight we have into the parenting lives of people we don't know. There are people I follow (on social media, I mean, not literally) who I will probably never meet. I don't *know* them, and they certainly don't know me. Yet I *feel like* I know them. If I saw them in the street, I would recognise them as if they were an old friend. I would recognise their kids. I know what car they drive, what pram they push, their dress size, whether or not they had a forceps-assisted delivery and what colour they've convinced Gary/Paul/[insert Instahusband] to paint the bathroom.

I have also experienced the flip side of this sharing relationship, bumping into people who've followed me from afar online who then greet me with the familiarity of a close relative. I have been hugged at the airport by someone who wanted to 'thank me for understanding her'. I was once intercepted at the supermarket as I was putting some baby food into my basket by a woman who said, 'Those dessert jars you've picked won't be great if Wilf's still got reflux, you need the thicker ones above.' Momentarily, I was confused. Did I know her? I was fairly sure I'd never seen her before in my life! Then I remembered, Wilf's reflux battles were public property. In fact, I have made all our lives public property by sharing what we're up to on Instagram and on Facebook. When I consider that broadcasting my innermost parenting thoughts and failures on the internet was the foundation of my blog and the driving force behind any social media engagement I've had, I realise that I am probably a professional sharent.

Yet even I believe that some people take it *too* far with the sharing, never more so than when parents share pictures of their kids' turds that look like particular shapes. If I get sent one more smiley shit or willy-shaped log, I'll have no choice but to get myself a dumbphone and renounce the internet. There is just no need.

# Sleeping Through

'Is he sleeping through yet?'

No, he isn't. Piss off.

# Supermum

Supermum has kitchen surfaces so clean you could lick them, due to her seven-scrubs-a-day Zoflora habit (#hinching). She has perky breasts, ultra-super-duper skinny jeans, a glowy complexion from her morning spinning class and the arse of a 16-year-old cheerleader. She is most often seen sporting a jumper with a positive message ('mumpreneur') and to unwind in the evenings she listens to podcasts about how best to organise her time, something she has the time to do because she already successfully organises her time. Supermum is everything you are not and will haunt you in your dreams, preying on your parental insecurities.*

· · · · · · · · · · · · ·

\* Supermum is a fictional character and any resemblance to persons living or dead is purely coincidental.

# Teething

'Oh dear, is he teething?' This seems to be the standard question we are asked whenever we are standing in a checkout queue with a grizzly baby and, to be honest, the answer is always 'Afraid so.'

It feels like Wilf has been teething constantly since the day he was born. OK, that might be a slight exaggeration, but he's certainly been teething since he was around three months old, when he first decided to stick a whole fist in his mouth then gum frantically on it. The cuffs of his sleepsuits are always soaking from incessant chewing and we get through at least five 'dribble bibs' a day, which he saturates by trying to get a wider variety of objects in his gob. He went through a stage of taking his socks off while in his car seat, sucking them, then falling asleep so that, when we arrived at our destination, we'd find him barefoot with two soggy socks in his lap.

We bought him several teethers to try and curb his fixation with gumming on his clothes, and his 'My Friend Goo' teether was a big hit for a while, until Wilf discovered it was fun to lob his friend Goo into the road from the pram, which resulted in several dicey Goo-rescues during the school run and prompted us to revert to allowing sock-chewing.

Teething is, unfortunately, just one of those things you have to grin (ha) and bear. You can throw money at granules (short-term saviour) or amber teething necklaces (zero evidence they work, but Suzy from the cloth-nappy café says they do) but, really, you just have to ride it out.

It would be much easier if babies were just born with a full set of teeth to begin with. That said, it would be terrifying. Imagine being handed a tiny newborn for the first time then seeing them flash a Hollywood smile. Nope. Teething misery it is.

# Tidying Up

When you have kids, attempting to tidy up is like pissing against the wind. There is, quite honestly, little point.

I can spend an entire day cleaning and tidying – believe it or not, I value having a smart, presentable home – yet within minutes the hard work will be undone by the kids and I'm left wondering whether we'd all be happier if we just embraced living in squalor instead. Imagine the time I would get back.

T

Firstly, there are all the toys. It doesn't matter how many times we try and 'rationalise' them, they seem to breed. I have always been very firm in my conviction that we mustn't spoil our children, yet the overflowing toy shelves and baskets suggest that's another parenting intention that's nose-dived. There are a great many decent toys that I don't mind at all, plus books, which I don't believe you can ever have too many of, but then there's all the *crap*. Tiny pieces of plastic shit that don't seem to belong to anything, yet if I ask the kids, they'll tell me it's part of a Thunderbirds set they got four years ago (and of course they need it).

Henry and Jude's bedroom is the worst offender, and walking in to see a toy explosion, minutes after I've tidied up, is a real red-mist trigger. I don't even have particularly high standards for what 'tidy' means in their room either; it would just be nice to occasionally see the carpet and avoid ending up in A&E again. I thought I'd come up with a good system by buying them each an under-bed storage box from Ikea then instructing them to bung everything from the middle of the floor into their boxes when they've finished playing. I'm not going to audit what's *inside* the boxes, I told them. Just shove everything in there and then push the boxes under the beds so I don't have to see the mess. It felt like a fair compromise. What's actually happened, however, is that those 'under-bed' boxes now sit among the piles of crap in the centre of the room and, what's more, the little hooligans have managed to stand on the lids and crack them. Every now and again I'll scream a bit, and a few times I've marched in armed with black bin bags and threatened to take 'the whole bloody lot to the charity shop tomorrow', but they've come to recognise a heat-of-the-moment empty threat when they see one so they don't bat an eyelid.

Then there's the bathroom. We finally have a bathroom I'm happy with (it's got a fancy cast-iron bath in it and everything;

I love it as much as I love the kids), yet said kids have zero respect for its fanciness. Cleaning the bathroom involves repeatedly removing toothpaste from wherever they have smeared it (predominately the windowsill, though occasionally the taps and radiator), and that's before I've even started with the state they leave the toilet in.

One would assume, upon examining the evidence, that my boys do their stand-up wees blindfolded. I did ask James to teach them how to do it properly (something I'm sadly not qualified to do), and it would appear he took them to a fairground and showed them a drunk person having a go at shooting rubber ducks with a water pistol. Even sit-down wees can be problematic as, in their haste to get back to playing with toys they'll never put away, they forget to shuffle back enough and I discover, the next time I clean the toilet, a dried pool of wee that has collected under the rim of the seat. #Blessed.

My third and final bugbear, to complete my tidying-up woe, is the boys' failure to put their dirty clothes in the washing basket, which results in me stepping over dirty jeans and pants which are generally inside out and still intertwined, having been taken off as one. Sometimes they will be left in the middle of the landing or on the stairs, so I'm met with a pant-over-trouser as I make my way up to bed, and every now and again there will be a skid-mark situation, which is nothing to be ashamed about when you are learning to navigate the toilet properly but I'd still rather not have that part of the pants staring at my face. Something I wouldn't have to endure if they put their clothes in the washing basket.

The very best thing I can recommend, should you feel your house needs a good old clean and tidy, is to prime a friend to come over at some point with only half an hour's notice. It's amazing what you can get done when you know you're having visitors. In fact, I'd recommend a panic clean over spending all day Sunday properly organising stuff. You know the kids aren't going to respect your sorting and labelling, anyway. Don't torture yourself.

# Toddlers

I was doing some work in a café last summer when a little girl, who must have been around two, came in with her dad. He'd popped in to fix the WiFi connection, so got her a chocolate brownie and left her to it while he attempted to sort out the internet. What happened next was the purest, most beautiful display of 'toddlerness' I have probably ever seen.

She'd been given a little spoon, as it was one of those soft, gooey brownies that you can't easily pick up. She soon realised, however, that the spoon was a bit of a faff so she started to use her fingers to break up the brownie. The more it broke up, the more she had to kind of grab at it, until she was using both her hands as little scoops and sort of shovelling it into her mouth, smearing chocolate all over her chin and dropping crumbs on to the chair and the floor below in the process. I found myself transfixed, smiling from ear to ear, as I watched her finish the last of her treat, closing her eyes to really savour the taste before she finally picked up the plate and *licked* it clean, oblivious to the giggles of the other customers, me included, who were so enjoying her brownie appreciation. Despite the obvious crumb carnage caused, there was something relaxing about watching the way she had zoned out of everything else to focus solely on eating that brownie. She had no idea that anyone was watching her, no worry about what she looked like. She had one thing and one thing only on her mind, and it was almost *meditative*. What a little legend.

It got me thinking that maybe toddlers get a bad rap when, actually, all things considered, they're pretty awesome. When someone says 'toddler' we think of tantrums, meltdowns and potty-training mishaps. We remember all the times our toddlers have dug their heels in and refused to get into the shopping trolley, arching their backs and contorting into a plank shape that cannot be squeezed into the seat. We remember, too, the frustrating stage when they want to do everything for themselves but also still want you to do everything for them, which usually manifests itself in their insistence that they want to walk somewhere 'like a big boy/girl' before conceding ten steps later that they'd be better off 'having a little carry', all the way to town and back. There's no denying that toddlers can be tossers.

Yet between their moments of infuriating irrationality, toddlers are an inspiration to us all. They find joy in all the simple things that we, as adults, have forgotten how to feel joyful about. They sing and dance in public. They don't hold back on their glee if they love something. They don't bother with bullshit if they don't like something. They don't hold a grudge. They don't care if someone is judging them, and haven't yet learned to judge themselves. They basically give zero fucks, which is absolutely glorious when it comes to eating a messy chocolate brownie in a busy café.

Life is short. Eat the cake, lick the plate. Be more toddler.

# Tummy Time

Placing your baby on their stomach during the daytime, when they're awake and you can supervise, is something you're advised to start doing pretty much immediately. Sold to me by the baby books as something that would be not only a pleasurable part of our daily routine but also vital in helping my

baby strengthen his neck and shoulder muscles *and* help with motor skills (win–win!) I was excited to get tummy-timing.

Alas, none of my boys greatly enjoyed tummy time and, in fact, both Henry and Wilf (I am noticing a pattern as I write this book that sees Jude as the respite in the middle) screamed blue bloody murder the *moment* they were placed on their fronts, in part, largely, we think, to their reflux and the fact it was never long before they spewed their latest feed on the special tummy-time mat I'd bought with mirrors and ducks on.

We persisted because I was petrified with both of them that we'd end up with a flat-headed baby (noting the advice that they should sleep on their backs, tummy time is also offered as a way to give the baby a break from constantly having their head laying against something). Every day it was the same charade, with me getting to ground level in denial about the fact that tummy time was simply never going to be in favour.

I am pleased (and somewhat relieved) to report that none of the boys has a flat head and their motor skills don't appear to have been severely impacted, though I'll never know if the lack of tummy time in their formative years will hold them back from reaching their full potential. I think I can just about live with that guilt.

# Underqualified

Every new parent will feel underqualified for the role. Even not-new parents will feel underqualified at times. That's because, well, it's because we *are* underqualified. In fact, we're completely *un*qualified. It's the biggest and most important job you will ever take on and yet nobody insists you do a diploma or a conversion course first. There's no apprenticeship pathway or two weeks' work experience during the school holidays. On the contrary, you accept a lifelong position, the hours being full time, seven days a week, 365 days a year, with zero experience of a similar role and no formal training.

That said, if you could do a three-year comprehensive parenting degree or even a four-year one with a gap-year placement looking after a toddler in Spain, no one would have kids, would they? Perhaps the lack of qualifications fuels the mystery needed to keep people having babies. *How hard can it be?* and then BOOM. Surprise!

The reassuring thing is that, aside from Mary Poppins, nobody else could be more qualified to care for your children than you are. The on-the-job training is the best you can get. Think of it as a fast-track scheme.

# Undervalued

You will also feel this.

# Unpaid

And this.

# Vagina

Fanny. Foo-foo. Muff. Lady garden. Whatever you call yours, if a baby or babies have come out of it, the chances are your relationship with it will have changed.*

. . . . . . . . . . . . .

* The relationship with your vagina might also have changed if a baby (or babies) came out of the sunroof, but I have no C-section experience to write from, other than a second-hand account from a friend, who told me, 'My fanny may be intact but my mind isn't. I don't think I've been touched down there since she [the baby] was conceived!'

# V

Mine has changed for the better. The relationship I mean, not the actual vagina, which in all honesty doesn't look quite as good as it did before three humans emerged from it.

In the earliest days of motherhood I felt sorry for it. I vividly remember, a couple of days after Henry was born, doing exactly what I'd been advised against doing and positioning a mirror underneath it to 'assess the damage'. I don't know what I was expecting a post-birth vagina to look like, but it wasn't *that*. It looked so tragic. As though it had been beaten up, left for dead and had then formed a frowny face around the outside edges using bits I was certain had once been on the inside. I whispered my apologies to it and then tucked it safely inside one of those jumbo-length maternity pads, vowing to nurse it back to health. A new-found kindness and respect had been born for the muscular canal that had itself allowed something rather special to be born. 'Aren't vaginas incredible?!' I said to James. 'Think how *big* it had to go!'

With the benefit of hindsight, reminding my husband how far things had stretched probably wasn't helpful in encouraging him to disassociate what he had seen in the delivery suite from what we'd previously enjoyed in the bedroom, but then it's safe to say his relationship with my vagina has changed, too. Around seven weeks after Wilf was born (warning: skip this section if you're eating your cornflakes), I became convinced I had a vaginal prolapse because of the ever-worsening feeling of heaviness and pressure inside my foof. In fact, having self-diagnosed that a prolapse was the most likely problem via the friend/foe that is Google, I made James take a look to tell me once and for all whether there was indeed surplus tissue protruding where it shouldn't be. His exact words, as he sat on the sofa with my crotch at his eye level while I kind of thrust my fanny at his face, as if I were performing a really threatening lap dance, was 'It looks fine ... if a little bulgy.' *Bulgy!* Good God,

# V

it was happening. Several hours, some mirror evaluation and plenty more googling later, I'd retracted my self-diagnosis and it seemed more likely that the sensation of heaviness and pulling I'd been experiencing was instead due to a large clot that had formed and was finally on its way out. What happened next (seriously, put the cornflakes down) was actually a bit scary. I realised, after a bit of pushing on the loo, that said clot was not going to dislodge itself easily and so instinct took over and I found myself on the bathroom floor, kind of straddling the bath mat, where I 'birthed' a surprisingly large clump of gunk from my uterus, several weeks after all the other bleeding had stopped.* If you want to pinpoint the greatest 'for better or for worse' moment of our marriage to date (superseding the time James had to milk me), then me shouting, 'Babe, it came out! Can you come up and have a look?' is a strong contender. I needed to share it with someone and, God love him, an ashen-faced James was there.

Giving birth and the subsequent moments of fanny-drama have left me feeling generally uninhibited when talking about my vagina. It's liberating. I never thought of myself as a prude before I had kids, but I was definitely a lot more private about my privates and I certainly didn't have as much respect for it as I do now. It existed for under-the-covers action and, once a month, I did the essential menstrual management. That was it, really. There was no real love shown for it (aside from the obvious). And now? Well, now I am kinder to it. I am better acquainted with it and I am committed to looking after its health, longer term. Whereas the prospect of a smear test might, in the past, have been a daunting one, nowadays it's

* FYI, you should always get checked out if you pass clots larger than a golf ball, or if anything else is giving you cause for concern.

197

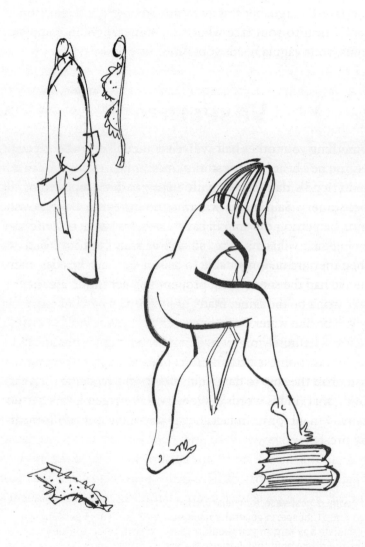

something I'll happily schedule between the school run and Turtle Tots. If you're due yours and have been putting it off, please book it. It's just as important and no more awkward than an eye test – arguably, less awkward, at least nobody breathes heavily next to your face while they shine a light in your eyes – plus, your vagina needs you. As do your kids.

# Vasectomy

Something your other half will tell you he'll 'never be getting' because he's heard horror stories from his mates about a friend of a friend's dad whose willy ballooned up and exploded post-surgery. Said mates will note that they themselves will never be getting the snip because they are going to continue sowing their wild oats – the full oaty version – until such a time when they are no longer able to deliver the oats. Besides, men who've had the snip are not proper men any more, are they?

'It won't be the same, mate!'

'It'll be like water.'*

'You'll definitely regret it. What if you want more kids?'

The last point is actually the main reason Mr Unmumsy hasn't had the snip to date, but I think 2020 could be the year, noting that (in his words), 'We've already got at least one too many.' I'm all for it. In fact, I might arrange one as his birthday present.

. . . . . . . . . . . .

* I googled 'post-vasectomy ejaculation' (all in a day's work) and discovered that sperm generally makes up no more than 5 per cent of ejaculate anyway, so you shouldn't notice any difference. I then read on and discovered that, because the sperm can no longer fire out in the moment of ecstasy, they disintegrate and are reabsorbed by the body. Nice little thought, that.

# Washing

Washing is *The NeverEnding Story* for parents. I know we voluntarily entered into a lifetime of laundry by having three children, all of whom have had reflux, which further ruined our chances of ever being truly on top of the washing situation, but even with the additional puking, I could never have forecast that a family of five would produce such an astronomical turnover of dirty clothes. I feel like I need to cut down on my work hours and spend a good two days a week just washing, drying and putting them away. I'm always quite good at the washing part – it's so easy to bung a load on and often it's the first thing I do, when I'm full of good intentions for the day ahead. Then life

happens and the clean washing sits in the machine for a day or two until it smells like a fish tank that needs cleaning and has to be re-washed. In good weather, particularly those first bright and breezy days of spring, I'm all over the drying task. I'd go so far as to say I enjoy hanging the sheets out – never am I more smug than when I'm taking advantage of good drying weather – but drying days are few and far between and, more often than not, it starts to rain, so I half-heartedly shove a few towels and pairs of socks over radiators, where they remain damp.

Worse than the washing and the drying is the backlog of clean washing that never gets put away. We have a floordrobe, a doordrobe and a chairdrobe. On a standard weekday morning, when I'm running around like a tit in a trance trying to get everyone and everything ready, it is almost guaranteed that I will be taking clean clothes for the kids straight from one of the many 'to be put away' piles that litter our bedroom and the landing, because they've not made it back into drawers. These laundry piles remain my nemesis and probably will do for the foreseeable future, though I did buy a couple of fancy baskets for our bedroom to put them in as a stop-gap destination before the drawers they'll never reach – so at least my washing sloth-fulness will be Instagrammable.

I'm trying to think of the last time we were completely up to date on the washing front – I mean, everything washed, dried *and* put away – and I think it was September 2016, when Henry started school and I turned over a new leaf and vowed to be a super-organised school mum. It lasted about three days and then Jude wet the bed, which meant my wash-dry-fold schedule went to shit and I never got back on track.

I'll tell you this, though, as long as you promise not to tell anyone. Very recently, I found myself looking at the ginor-mous mountain of garments on our bedroom floor and having a bit of a moment. The heap of clothes had previously been folded in some sort of order on the bed. Henry and Jude had decided, though, that they wanted to use the bed as a boat in a game of 'shark fishing' so had swept the clothes aside and on to the floor. As I gazed at the messy mound, I saw the clothes not for what they represented in terms of workload but what they said about this moment in our lives. Football socks from a seven-year-old who thinks he's going to be a pro, endless jumpers from a four-year-old who wipes his nose on his sleeve, sleepsuits with orange-stained collars from a baby who can't get enough of his carrot puffs, and grown-up clothes stained with paint and floor varnish as we try our best to do up our doer-upper. Will I ever miss having to wade through mountains of washing to get into bed? Absolutely not. But I reckon there'll come a time when I'll miss the period of our lives that brought with it the most chaos and, consequently, the most washing.

# Whingeing

Moaning. Griping. Whining. Grumbling. The soundtrack to life with small children. Some days, it's more of a background hum, a din of general dissatisfaction beneath whatever else is going on.

> They don't want to go where you have told them you're going.
>
> They do want to go to where you have told them you're not going.
>
> They hate pesto pasta, even though last night they complained that their jacket potato wasn't pesto pasta.
>
> They're tired.

They can't believe you're forcing them to have a bath.

The blue pen isn't red.

And so on. This level of continuous whinge is annoying, but it's tolerable – after a while, you learn to tune out and very often it's not until the little terrors are in bed that you realise you've had an unbroken whinge ringing in your ears all day.

On other days, it's less a background noise and more of a hurricane-level whinge. What prompts these more severe whinge days is unclear, though I'm inclined to believe that children can smell their parents' desperation and turn the whinge dial up accordingly. This means that whenever there is important shit going on and Mummy and Daddy could really do without having to pause their grown-up problem-solving, they are forced to calm down a toddler who is whinge-ing to let them know he is deeply insulted by the 'bits' he's found in his drink, despite them explaining several times that those bits are, in fact, his own backwash from snogging rather than sipping from the bottle when he's midway through a mouthful of sandwich.

Perhaps there's a correlation between intense whinge levels and a full moon, or perhaps it's simply par for the parenting course that every so often children wake up and decide they will hate everything the day throws at them from the moment they get out of bed – on your marks, get set, whinge. One thing that is certain is that those whingefest parenting days can be some of the toughest and most challenging of all, particularly if you have two or more children whose whinge barometers are synched to peak at the same time. Throw the snivel of a teething and clingy baby into the mix and it's only a matter of time before you'll start fantasising about silence, darkness and Anadin.

The most bizarre thing about all this whingeing, at least when it comes to my own children, is how extraordinarily disproportionate their reactions seem to the situation/food/ incident they've taken a dislike to. I know I can never truly understand how something has made my children feel and therefore perhaps it is wrong of me to pass judgement on whether their instinct to moan is *disproportionate* or not. I have, after all, been told off in the past for commenting that my children are 'being ridiculous' when they are having a meltdown, most notably by a woman on Instagram who told me I was undermining their self-expression. The problem is that, although I'm all for encouraging my children's self-expression, there are times when they self-express themselves as dickheads.

Only recently, as I embarked on a quick trip to the shops with Henry in tow (to buy a birthday present for one of *his* friends, for one of *his* friends' birthdays), what started as a base level of muttering about how bored he was escalated quickly and culminated in him dropping to the floor as though he'd been taken out by a sniper when I mentioned we needed to 'quickly pop into one more shop' for the card. He *was* being ridiculous, and I will stand by that until my dying day.

# Willies

'Don't dip your willy in your yoghurt.'
'You really shouldn't pull the skin like that, it's not Stretch Armstrong.'
'Leave your brother's pecker alone.'
'Who wiped their willy on the sofa?'
'I'm being serious now, put it away. The waiter is coming over to take our order.'

With three boys in the house, the willy-related warnings are endless. It feels like I'm permanently talking about willies or telling somebody off for improper willy conduct. If I'm not instructing them to cease sword-fighting with their penises, or at the very least to downgrade their *Gladiator*-style attacks to a more graceful fencing manoeuvre, I'm reminding them to shake after having a wee, knowing as I do now that failure to do so results in them walking around with fishy-smelling dribble patches in their pants. (If you've never done the sniff-test to see if a pair of boys' pants are clean, I would suggest you keep it that way, or you're risking having the aroma of uncooked spoiled seafood up your nostrils for days.)

Some days it feels like I'm fighting a losing battle just to keep penises under wraps, and that's excluding the half an hour before bed when we're treated to the 'willy show', as my over-tired and hyperactive children refuse to put on their pyjamas and instead jiggle their willies from side to side *à la* Ricky Martin in 1999.

Heaven help me when they become teenagers, though with any luck the constant willy-flicking won't still be taking place communally in front of *The One Show*.

# Wind

Wind is one of the most, if not *the* most, ridiculous things about human babies. Something's gone awry in the evolutionary process when it comes to winding, surely? I know there are probably reasons why human babies are so helpless – in fact, I'm sure I read an article once about how babies' prolonged helplessness has a cognitive pay-off in the long run, i.e. yes, it takes them ages to do anything independently, but all the while their brains are developing to have complex thinking. Which is great and everything – I get the message and I'm certainly not suggesting babies should be born and then walk straight off to the Job Centre – but for the love of God, it's time they learned to burp themselves.

When I was pregnant for the first time, the actual motion of winding a baby, those little rubs and back-pats, was one of the things I pictured myself lovingly doing. I'd been out for coffee with a friend and her little boy previously, and she'd said, 'Can you just give him a little wind for me while I go to the loo?' I'd sat there patting his tiny back, feeling like a natural. There didn't seem to be a lot to it.

What nobody had warned me about was how that feed-wind-burp cycle would take over my entire life and that, sometimes, I would find myself pacing the floorboards with a screaming baby, trying everything in my power to soothe him when all he really needed was a fart. Occasionally, you hit the jackpot and get a baby who only seems to need a small pat of encouragement to bring up a burp. Jude was like that, which is why he's my favourite.

For everyone else, winding becomes its own sport. There are tips, such as how best to sit them/where to rub them; tricks, such as bicycle-pumping their little legs; and products, for when you're really desperate. We were always really desperate so we stockpiled everything available, including Infacol, which others swear by but which we nicknamed Doesfuckall, and gripe water. If you've got a baby the same age as my Henry and were using gripe water to help bring up wind, you will almost certainly remember the Great Gripe Water Shortage of 2012. For some reason, manufacturing had come to a halt and parents were advised to only buy what they needed and not stockpile bottles, as more would be on their way soon. I read and understood that advice but decided, all things considered, that I just couldn't risk it. I went on a frenzied tour of mid-Devon chemists and ended up buying enough bottles to last him until he was sixteen. I hid them at the back of the airing cupboard, as though I were anticipating getting raided. Hormones will do that to you.

Sometimes, the winding takes just as long or even longer than the feed itself and, if you have a baby with reflux, the result of the winding is inevitable. I remember one evening, not long after baby Wilf was born, putting him down in his cot straight after a feed. Without winding. As our third baby, we really should have known better, but I think perhaps it was *because* he was our third that we'd become a bit cocky. We were now rule-breakers, casual about the parenting should-dos. He'd fallen asleep lying on my boob and it was just so easy to transfer him in that same position straight to the cot, ready for what we were sure would be a mammoth sleep stint.

It was two minutes before he started fussing and, the moment I picked him up, he projectile vomited like Regan in *The Exorcist*, all over our shutters. We never cut winding corners again.

# Witching Hour

The hour or two before bedtime that turns children into screaming banshees. With Henry and Jude, chaos kick-off was generally sometime between 5 and 7 p.m., but with Wilf, the witching hour quite often starts as early as 4 p.m., which, in all honesty, is a fresh hell we weren't prepared for.

I have grown used to making excuses for my children when this happens (and it happens a lot). Usually it's that they're 'overtired' or 'overwhelmed'. Just recently, I heard myself say, 'I think it's all just got a bit too much,' to explain the behaviour of all three boys – who were wailing after Henry and Jude had bumped heads doing the Hype dance from *Fortnite*, knocking

Wilf over in the process – before realising how ridiculous that was. What can possibly get 'too much' in the life of seven-, four- and one-year-olds to justify them stripping naked, shouting and generally behaving like tiny delinquents just as I'm about to serve up tea? I'd understand if they had the weight of the world on their shoulders, feeling stressed about finding a good time to book the car in for a service, or anxious about the never-ending Things to Do list circling in their heads, the implications of Brexit, the environmental impact of single-use plastics and whether there would be enough money to buy everyone Christmas presents. Even then, it's not really an *excuse*, is it? I'm regularly at my wits' end for all sorts of reasons, but you rarely find me stripping down to my pants, screaming at the top of my lungs and getting aggressive because somebody's sitting where I wanted to sit on the sofa.

The craziest thing about the witching hour is that it can ruin an otherwise pleasant day. Those days when you feel like you are winning at parenting because you've been out for a walk and the children have returned with rosy cheeks and muddy boots, the sort of days when you take loads of pictures because you want to capture the beauty of being out as a family and simply can't imagine your life without them #mykidsmyworld. It takes just minutes for the fresh air and delight of quality family time to be replaced by a brawl over whose turn it is to play with Buzz Lightyear, a protest about whatever is on the menu for dinner and the screams of a baby who wants to come up for a cuddle but as soon as he's up for a cuddle wants to get back down again (repeat until he goes to bed).

When people talk about having nannies and au pairs I often think, *That sounds nice*, but to be honest, all I really want is a witching-hour nanny. Someone to come in at 4.30 p.m., make the kids their tea, mediate fights and say, 'Can we all just calm down a bit?' in a slightly less desperate tone to the one I normally use. That said, if I'd had one of those from the outset, I probably wouldn't be writing this book, as half the material has been inspired by events that have unfolded during those 'testing' hours. I bet divorces unfold during those hours, too.

Do kids grow out of it? Do other people's kids wind down nicely before bed? Is there any way to curtail the witching-hour madness? Help me.

# Worry

I once saw a congratulations-on-the-new-baby card which read, 'When a baby is born, a mother is also born.' It was a lovely sentiment and I totally get what it was trying to say, but I can't help but feel it needs tweaking. The reason I think it needs tweaking is that nothing has made me feel more like a mother than the amount of time I spend worrying, and that worry kicked in the second I found out I was pregnant with Henry, not the second he was born.* I do, however, understand that 'When you wee on a stick and it tells you you're pregnant, a mother is born' probably doesn't have quite the same ring to it. Regardless, the moment you know there is someone in there, you become a worrier.

In fact, when you become a parent, the very nature of how you worry and what you worry about completely changes. Any worry you once had for yourself is completely eclipsed by the worries you start to have for your child. In the hierarchy of worrying, your own needs and ailments fall right to the

· · · · · · · · · · · ·

\* I also think it is problematic to make birth the moment someone 'becomes a mother' when there are many women who lose babies in pregnancy – they are already mothers and to say otherwise is insensitive (though I realise it wasn't a card aimed at bereaved mothers).

bottom of the pile. I can remember being told by doctors with concerned faces that I had pre-eclampsia when I was in labour with Henry. Everything they then said about how serious it was for my health was white noise. I was aware of worrying blood-pressure readings and snippets of conversation about a risk of fitting, but the whole time I had only one worry in my head. *Was the baby OK?*

Those 'Is the baby OK?' worries are constant. When the twelve-week scan arrives and you sit in the waiting room watching other couples depart with their scan photos, the excitement of seeing your baby for the first time gives way to a little bit of fear. The more we're exposed to other parents' stories on social media, the more we come to realise that it isn't always plain sailing and that, actually, taking a healthy baby home at the end of the journey isn't the way the story unfolds for everybody. By the time I was having a twelve-week scan for my second baby, I had read lots more stories about missed miscarriages and not finding a heartbeat, so think I had a greater sense of worry than I'd had the first time around. I sat with knotted fingers, praying that my little pip would be found safe in there.

At thirty-seven weeks pregnant with Wilf, I realised I hadn't felt him move for a while and the worry I felt gradually crept up from being fairly mild, where I drank a glass of icy water, prodded my tummy and lay down in different positions in an attempt to get him to kick, to high, where I called the midwife to say I couldn't feel any movement, then called James and we went straight to hospital, where I was hooked up to a machine which told us, with a reassuring print-out of graph paper, that Wilf was simply just having a lazy day.

Even when your child has arrived safely, I bet there isn't a parent on earth who hasn't at some stage accidentally woken their peacefully sleeping baby by prodding them to check that they're still breathing. Or sat watching for the rise and fall of a little chest, afraid to not watch, to not check. I thought it would get easier as they got older – that the anxiety would lessen, but if anything, I worry more now than I did when I had new babies, I just worry about different things.

In hindsight, the early worry I had about being solely – well, jointly – responsible for the safety and wellbeing of a small person turned out to be less intense than the worries I now have about all the times my babies are not with me, when I have no control whatsoever of their safety and wellbeing (even though I know logically that, even as babies, their overall wellbeing was never 100 per cent within my control).

I've replaced worries about what could happen when my baby is sleeping with worries about what could happen when my baby is at nursery. *Is he getting enough milk?* has morphed into *I hope he says no to grapes unless they're cut in half, lengthways.* Worries about when my children will start walking and talking have become worries about why they're being quiet, are they happy, how would I know if they are being bullied?

I am reliably informed by friends who have teenagers or grown-up children that this will only get worse as they get older and said 'control' over their safety and wellbeing continues to diminish even further. I can well believe it. Just the thought of my boys getting the bus into town with mates, going to parties where people offer them pills or passing their driving tests and being let loose on the roads of Devon, alone, is enough to make my worry gauge burst.

One thing I have learned is that, as a parent, you'll come to distinguish larger, deeper worries that you know you ought to act on from those general parenting niggles you'll never shift and will simply have to live with – 'Feel the fear and do it anyway,' or something like that. For us, the sense of unease I felt when Henry was invited to go somewhere without us, with a family we knew very little about, was enough for me to say, 'Thank you so much for the invite, but I'm not comfortable with this situation unless myself or my husband comes, too.' Whereas the worry I have about him choking when I'm not there is something I can only alleviate by teaching him to sit down and chew properly when he's eating (and never eat a whole grape), then hoping for the best. I still worry, but maybe slightly less so.

Worrying definitely comes with the job.

# Xmas

Truth be told, I hate it when people abbreviate 'Christmas' to 'Xmas'. It's pure laziness, only excusable in the late nineties or early noughties, when you had a character limit on text messages so spoke lyk u woz drunk lol. However, I'm hoping that maybe, just maybe, it's also excusable when you're writing an A–Z and the X section is looking a bit sorry for itself. I will endeavour to earn your forgiveness for this slovenly use of language by calling it Christmas henceforth.

I've realised, as I have got further into this book, that when it comes to making observations about most areas of parenting, I have a habit of outlining all the expectations I had, pre-parenthood, then one by one blowing them to bits with the realities of what actually unfolded. That's kind of my trademark, and it's what comes most naturally to me, simply because it's the truth: in my experience, there is a massive chasm of disappointment between expectation and reality, and that's not because the reality is shit – far from it! – but rather because our expectations are overinflated to begin with, misinformed by the airbrushed version of parenting we're exposed to on social media, in films and in magazines. There are a few exceptions to that rule, however, and the biggest and most notable non-disappointment of the parenting experience to date has been Christmas, which has met every great expectation I had for it and then some, which is hugely impressive, noting that, on a personal level, the stakes were extremely high.

I needed Christmas to be good, I think. I was the biggest lover of Christmas growing up, and I have happy memories of staring at twinkling Christmas-tree lights and bounding into my mum and dad's room alongside my sister on Christmas morning, jumping on their bed to open our stockings (in hindsight, it was a bit of a scandal that Father Christmas never once wrapped any of our stocking presents, like he did our friends', but at the time, it was no less magic). If I close my eyes, I can go right back to the warmth of the kitchen, the smell of oranges, Mum's rosy face flushed from preparing the dinner, Dad wearing his new M&S slippers, which were the same as the ones he'd got the previous ten years, and the sound of Slade on the radio. Christmas to me was when we felt the most like a family. It was warm, fuzzy, safe and full of chocolate, some of which we were allowed to eat before breakfast, the ultimate treat.

On Boxing Day 2002, however, the unthinkable happened to our Christmas bubble when we lost Mum to breast cancer. I was fifteen. It felt so wrong, so wicked, that all around us the lights kept twinkling and the sleighbell-filled songs kept playing when Mum had gone. I'd gone all out on a super-snazzy pair of slippers for her that year, a real treat for when she was better and could come home from hospital, but of course she hadn't come home from hospital, so they lay unopened under the tree. It was, in many ways, a sliding-doors moment for Christmas. It would have been easy to fall out of love with Christmas, to hear Slade and remember only the heartbreak of knowing Mum would never again put on a silly hat and dance around the kitchen to it, but I didn't want that for Christmas. I didn't want the tragedy of that year to overwrite the other years that had made me fall in love with Christmas in the first place and so I made a vow to myself that I would do my best to continue to enjoy Christmas, with the bigger picture always in my mind: one day I would have children of my own and what a legacy it would be for my mum if I was able to re-create the warm, fuzzy, safe and full-of-choc-olate Christmas environment for her grandchildren.

By and large, that is exactly how Christmas feels again and, as someone who openly finds so much of parenting a chal-lenge, it's the one time of year when it all comes good. There is even more to love about Christmas than there was before kids came along and, let's be honest, the same can't always be said for other special occasions during the year, can it? Birthdays are most notably a bit rubbish once you have kids.

'Can you wipe my bum, Mum?'
'NO, IT'S MY BIRTHDAY!'
'But it's a really messy one.'
FML.

That's not to say, of course, that Christmas isn't sometimes a teeny bit stressful, and I have at times felt overwhelmed by the festive task list that comes with it. I have also, on a small number of occasions, felt myself almost succumbing to the unnecessary pressure of keeping up with the Joneses, or Clauses, at Christmas, feeling myself falling into a vortex of inadequacy because I haven't made Hogwarts out of gingerbread or flown the boys to Lapland for a meet-and-greet with the big man and instead have paid a few quid at the school fete again for a male teacher/the caretaker/someone they found in the playground, whose stubble is peeping over the top of his fake beard. I say *almost* because I've been good thus far at having a word with myself, remembering that the kids don't need Christmas to be fancy for it to be special.

And special it is. Little faces excited as the decorations go up. Letters being written. Nativity lines being learned, Christmas films being watched, songs being sung. Sure, there are squabbles and tears and 'Why can't you just behave yourselves?' moments, just the same as there are in every month that isn't December, but it's *Christmas*, and at Christmas they have to pack it in because the elves are watching.

I am sure there are many things I have done 'wrong' as a parent – there is no handbook, after all – but if the boys grow up as I hope they will, remembering Christmases that were warm, fuzzy, safe and full of chocolate, I know I will at least have done something right.

Have you forgiven me for calling it Xmas yet?

# X-rated

As a parent, sex will happen when, and only when, the following conditions have been met:

- *There aren't any children in your bed.*
- *There aren't any children looking at you.*

- *There aren't any children on the other side of the door asking where their wrestling stickers are.*

- *There aren't any children snoring loudly (as reassuring as it is to know they are asleep, it's quite hard to get in the mood when you can hear a four-year-old snuffling his nose against Mummy Pig's little stick foot).*

- *You managed to steal three minutes to have a wash, at least of the necessary areas. I'm including teeth-brushing here, though it's probably not essential, as time restraints mean there is rarely any snogging.*

- *It's not Monday (nobody does it on a Monday, do they?).*

- *It's not January (same as Monday).*

- *You're not on your period.*

- *You're not worried about not being on your period.*

- *It isn't too cold.*

- *Nobody has a cold.*

- *You're not too tired.*

- *You're not too stressed.*

- *You haven't had a row about the dishwasher.*

- *You're not having to do the work you couldn't do during the day because one or more of your children were too poorly for school/nursery.*

- *Luther isn't on (just not the same on Catch-up; Twitter always spoils it).*

- *You're not sitting next to each other on the sofa in silence, glued to your smartphones.*

If all the above is in order, there's no stopping you. Enjoy!

# Yearning For ...

A full night's sleep, an uninterrupted dinner, an uninterrupted film, an uninterrupted poo, the chance to get ready for a night out, a *relaxing* holiday, a weekend to be a couple, a weekend to be yourself, a break from cooking dinner, a break from the school run, some fresh air on your own, a little taste of what life used to be like *before*.

It's perfectly OK to yearn for any, or all, of the above. *You are allowed*. It doesn't make you a terrible parent. It doesn't make you a terrible person. It doesn't mean that you hate having children. It doesn't mean that you regret having children. It doesn't mean you don't deserve to have children, and

it doesn't mean you preferred your life before you had children.

It means you're a human being who is trying your very best but sometimes feels close to burn-out and could do with a break. Loving your kids with all your heart and craving some time to be something other than 'Muuuuuuuuum' are not mutually exclusive states.

In the last seven years I have let far too many people shame me for admitting I'd like some time out or for daring to reminisce fondly about what life was like before the kids came along. It's a waste of worry, on my part, and a waste of shame on theirs. You shouldn't feel the need to apologise. Or explain yourself. If *you* know deep down that you are a good parent, you will also know that the odd yearn cannot blemish that.

Besides, yearning can lead to daydreaming, which is a good coping strategy when you find yourself at soft play in the school holidays. *Sunbathing in the Caribbean, sunbathing in the Caribbean, sunbathing in the Caribbean.* Someone's screaming for you from the ball pool. Back in the room.

# Yelling

One of the great many things you swore you wouldn't do but now do. Unfortunately, this behaviour is symptomatic of having kids who neither respect you nor listen to you and push your buttons regularly and unrelentingly.

When outside the safety of your own home, your full-throttle yell will reduce to a quieter, yet equally as angry, hiss. There might even be some growling, unless you're in Waitrose, where it is never appropriate to growl.

The worst time for yelling is the summer, when you forget the windows are open and screech-sob, 'THIS IS WHY WE

CAN'T HAVE NICE THINGS!' upon discovering permanent marker on your new cushion. There might even be an escaped F-bomb, something you are never proud of, but it was your best cushion and why do they have to be such savages? The yelling will scare poor Julie and Peter next door, who were relaxing on sun-loungers on their patio. At some point, you'll have to face them, usually when you tiptoe down the garden to peg the sheets on the line. They will pretend not to know that you know *they* know you allowed a 'fuck' to slip through the net while you were shrieking with the window open. 'All right, Julie? Yeah, we're all good, thanks. How about you guys?' Cringe.

# Zero Fucks

'Behold! The field in which I grow my fucks. Lay thine eyes upon it and thou shalt see that it is barren.'

– Nicked off the Internet, 2019

Though a difficult beast to get to grips with, if you *can* incorporate even a small slice of zero-fucks-given attitude into your parenting manifesto, it will change your life. Trust me.

Obviously, this is not advised when it comes to the broader, universally accepted aspects of parenting for which you *should* give a fuck – the safety and wellbeing of your children, not setting the house on fire, that sort of thing – but downgrading the amount you care about certain other things will be a game-changer for your wellbeing.

> What other people think you should be doing as a parent? Who cares?
>
> What other people don't think you should be doing as a parent? As above. What do they know?
>
> The fact that Instagram tells you yours is just about the only house remaining that hasn't been given the Marie Kondo treatment? Forget it. You have a houseful of objects that are neither useful nor spark joy. And that's just the kids.

The next time you find yourself worrying about something, or doubting yourself as a parent, ask yourself whether it's really something you should give two hoots about. If it isn't, don't! Don't even give it one hoot. Not really sure what a hoot is, but I'm certain you shouldn't give yours away so freely to things that don't deserve your hoots.

You are doing a great job. Remember that.

# Ze End

The eagle-eyed among you (waving at my editor!) will notice that alphabetically speaking, the previous entry should have been the final one, but the alternatives to this were: zoo, zorb-ing, zodiac or zonked and, while the latter is a superb fit with how I feel most of the time, a closing entry about how I'm really bloody tired, all of the time, just didn't seem punchy enough. (I am, though. So very tired.)

I mentioned at the beginning that this was to be the last *Unmumsy* book – three babies, three books; there is a certain neatness to it – so I guess all that remains is for me to say a huge thank-you to *you*, for picking up this book and reading it. Whether you've been there from the beginning or simply picked this book up when you did the supermarket Big Shop because you quite liked the cover, I am truly very grateful. What an adventure it has been.

Over and out, from our family to yours.

Sarah, James, Henry, Jude and Wilf
The Unmumsy Family

# Acknowledgements

Thank you to everyone at Transworld Publishers for making me feel like part of the team since 2015. When I grow up, I would like to work in your office, please. Special thanks to Michelle Signore, for being infectiously positive about all things Unmumsy Mum. Reviewing your edit notes, particularly when they mention bums and willies, is my favourite pastime. I'd also like to thank Alice Murphy-Pyle for coming up with clever marketing ideas and, with a heavier heart, I'd like to pay tribute to my publicist and friend Sophie Christopher, who we lost this year and whose infectious laugh is missed every day.

Alyana Cazalet, thank you for illustrating this book and bringing my words to life. This was my first experience of being illustrated and you were an absolute pleasure to work with.

# ACKNOWLEDGEMENTS

Hannah Ferguson, thank you for being an excellent sounding board and for going above and beyond by answering my panicked WhatsApp messages over Christmas when I decided I was never writing another word again.

I'm lucky to have a great many friends who have been there (and are always there!), but specifically for their support during the writing of *this* book, I would like to thank Emma Conway, for keeping me going with hilarious text messages, and Siobhan Miller, for offering 'you can do it' encouragement at the right time.

Dad, thank you for being the biggest fan of my work from the beginning, even when I was writing terrible stories and poems in exercise books. More recently, it is only with help from you, Tina, Ena and Andrew that I've had the headspace to work at all! Grandparents are amazing and I am so grateful for all you do for us.

To my boys: Henry, Jude and Wilf. What can I say? I love you beyond measure and I'm so proud to be your mummy. I'm only joking about writing *Unmumsy Reloaded: The Teenage Years* (probably).

Finally, and I have deliberately saved my biggest thanks until last, I would like to thank my husband and sanity-anchor, James. You are the yang to my yin – more level-headed than I am, less dramatic, and the person whose opinion I value above any other. You are also an exceptional father and the glue that holds our family together. If you stopped snoring and put your socks in the washing basket, you would be a 10/10.

# Resources

The following are some of the organisations that can provide support should you feel unable to cope, or think you might be suffering from postnatal depression.

Pandas Foundation
www.pandasfoundation.org.uk
0843 28 98 401

The Association for Postnatal Illness
apni.org
0207 386 0868

# RESOURCES

Cry-sis
www.cry-sis.org.uk
08451 228 669

NCT – The National Childbirth Trust
www.nct.org.uk

Samaritans
www.samaritans.org
116 123

Mind
www.mind.org.uk
0300 123 3393

**Sarah Turner** lives in Devon with her husband and their three boys. She started writing as The Unmumsy Mum after becoming disillusioned with the other parenting literature she had read online. Everybody seemed to be coping so well! Where were the tales of mums tearing their hair out after yet another sleepless night and endless re-runs of *Peppa Pig*? Surely there were others out there who were trying but ultimately failing to live up to the Supermum ideal they'd bought into? She made a vow then and there to document the good, the bad and the ugly of parenting and her blog (www.theunmumsymum.co.uk) was born. *The Unmumsy Mum* was voted number 4 in Amazon's Top 10 books of 2016 (as voted by Amazon customers) and was also shortlisted for Book of the Year (non-fiction, lifestyle) at the 2017 British Book Awards. You can follow Sarah's everyday parenting adventures on Facebook, Instagram and Twitter (@theunmumsymum).